**BIBLE STUDY
COMMENTARY**

COLOSSIANS AND PHILEMON

COLOSSIANS AND PHILEMON

BIBLE STUDY COMMENTARY

CURTIS VAUGHAN

ZONDERVAN
PUBLISHING HOUSE
OF THE ZONDERVAN CORPORATION | GRAND RAPIDS, MICHIGAN 49506

COLOSSIANS AND PHILEMON: BIBLE STUDY COMMENTARY
Copyright © 1973, 1980 by The Zondervan Corporation
Grand Rapids, Michigan

Library of Congress Cataloging in Publication Data

Vaughan, Curtis.
    Colossians and Philemon.

  Ed. for 1973 published under title: Colossians.
  Bibliography: p.
  1. Bible. N.T.   Colossians—Text-books.
2. Bible.   N.T.   Philemon—Commentaries.   I.   Title.
BS2715.5.V38   1980   227'.707   80-26772
ISBN 0-310-33583-3

Printed in the United States of America

Contents

**BIBLE STUDY
COMMENTARY**

**COLOSSIANS
AND PHILEMON**

CHAPTER 1

Background for the Study

Colossians, one of the shorter letters of the New Testament, has an importance and value out of all proportion to its size. But it is a difficult letter, with many obscure allusions to false teachings which are quite unfamiliar to the lay reader. Because of this Colossians is one of the relatively neglected books of the New Testament.

To enable us better to appreciate and comprehend its message it is appropriate that some consideration be given to the historical situation out of which the letter came and to which it was addressed. This we will do by looking at (1) the city, (2) the church, and (3) the epistle itself.

I. THE CITY OF COLOSSAE.

Colossae was a small town situated on the south bank of the Lycus River in the interior of the Roman province of Asia (an area included in modern Turkey). In earlier periods it had been, successively, a part of the kingdoms of Phrygia, Lydia, Persia, Greece, and Pergamum. The latter, in 133 B.C., bequeathed the region of Phrygia (which included Colossae) to Rome.

Colossae was located about a hundred miles east of Ephesus, its nearest neighbors being the cities of Laodicea (ten miles away) and Hierapolis (thirteen miles away). Both of these cities, the more important of which was Laodicea, are named in the epistle as having communities of believers (cf. 2:1; 4:13). The church at Laodicea, in fact, is mentioned as the recipient of an epistle from Paul (4:16). Colossae, though the smallest of the three in New Testament times, was older than either of the other two.

The fertile valley in which Colossae, Laodicea, and Hierapolis were located was in Paul's day a district of great wealth and had a large population. The area was probably the greatest center for the wool industry in the ancient world. Dyeing was also a significant feature of its economy.

In the ages of the Persian and Greek empires, Colossae, located on the main trade route linking Ephesus in the west and Persia in

9

the east, was a city of considerable importance. Both Herodotus (fifth century B.C.) and Xenophon (fourth century B.C.) bear testimony to this fact, the former calling Colossae "a great city of Phrygia" and the latter describing it as "a populous city, wealthy and large." But when the road system was later changed, Colossae's population began to diminish and eventually both Laodicea and Hierapolis surpassed it in position and wealth. Consequently, the Greek geographer Strabo, writing about two generations before Paul, could describe Colossae as "a small town." Kummel calls it "an insignificant market town" (p. 238).

In A.D. 60 or 61 Colossae, along with its neighboring cities, was devastated by an earthquake which resulted in terrible loss of life. It is somewhat surprising that Paul makes no allusion to this, for it was a calamity which profoundly impressed the whole empire and must have occurred only a short while before this epistle was written. Strabo observes that the entire district was volcanic and subject to earthquakes.

By A.D. 400 Colossae no longer existed as a city, and sometime around A.D. 700 the town was completely deserted. Its site is now but a place of ruins, the nearest town being the modern Honas.

The people who inhabited the area of Colossae, Laodicea, and Hierapolis in New Testament times fell into three groups: (1) the native Phrygians, (2) Greek colonists who came to live and trade there, and (3) Jews, the number of whom Barclay estimates to have been as high as 50,000.

II. The church at Colossae.

We have no record of the establishment of the Colossian church; indeed, Colossae is not even mentioned in Acts. All of our information about the church, therefore, must be derived from what is said in this letter. Three things may be mentioned:

1. *It was a Pauline church.* The person directly responsible for the founding of the Colossian church was not Paul but Epaphras (cf. 1:8; 2:1; 4:12, 13). The latter, however, was probably a convert of Paul and in the evangelization of Colossae was acting as a representative of the apostle (cf. 1:7, 8). The most probable date for the founding of the church is A.D. 53-55, during the time of Paul's Ephesian ministry (cf. Acts 19:10).

2. *It was a Gentile church.* There was, as stated above, a large Jewish population in the Lycus Valley, but the Colossian epistle represents the membership of the church as mainly Gentile (cf. 1:21, 27). In fact, Abbott feels "there is no hint that any of the readers were Jews" (p. xlviii).

3. *It was a troubled church.* Dangerous heresy had made an appearance in the Lycus Valley, and at the time of this letter was a serious threat to the well-being of the Colossian church. Since most of what is said in the epistle is related in some way to this false teaching, it is imperative that the reader learn as much about it as he can.

In the past, Biblical scholars have not agreed as to the identity of the "Colossian heresy." Some, for example Hort and Peake, contended that Jewish teaching could account for all of its diverse elements. Lightfoot, on the other hand, felt that it was an incipient form of Gnosticism reflecting Jewish (Essene) modifications. Others wanted to identify the heresy with the full-blown Gnosticism of the second century. There remain many unanswered questions, and much uncertainty must still be confessed, but there is considerable unanimity of opinion among present-day scholars. Indeed, Kummel observes that there are "hardly any differences in basic opinion" (p. 239).

The epistle does not give a direct account of the tenets of the Colossian heresy, and for that reason it is difficult for us to get a clear and consistent picture of it. However, from the many allusions to the heresy, we are able to sketch its leading features. Some of these are as follows:

(1) It professed to be a "philosophy" (2:8). But perhaps the word "theosophy" rather than "philosophy" more aptly describes the Colossian error. Moulton characterizes it as a "dabbling in the occult" (p. 3). Paul, refusing to recognize it as true philosophy, called it an "empty deceit" (cf. discussion of 2:8).

(2) It placed much emphasis on ritual circumcision, dietary laws, and the observance of holy days (2:11, 14, 16, 17).

(3) Affirming the mediation of various supernatural powers in the creation of the world, the work of redemption, and the whole process of salvation, the false teaching insisted that these mysterious powers be placated and worshiped (2:15, 18, 19). As a result of this, Christ was relegated to a relatively minor place in the Colossian system. "One thing," writes H. C. G. Moule, "is certain as to the 'Colossian Heresy.' It was a doctrine of God, and of salvation, which cast a cloud over the glory of Jesus Christ" .(p. 9).

(4) It was decidedly ascetic (2:20-23). The errorists of Colossae taught that the body is evil and must be treated as an enemy. All of its wishes must therefore be denied and its needs cut down to the barest minimum.

(5) The advocates of this system claimed to be Christian teachers but by smooth talk and specious arguments were attempting to draw the Colossians away from the truth (cf. 2:3-10).

From these considerations we may conclude that the Colossian heresy was a syncretistic system combining three separate elements. First, the insistence on legalism, ritualism, and the observance of holy days points to *a Jewish element.* However, it seems not to have been the Pharisaic Judaism combated in Galatians. Bruce calls it a "native Phrygian variety" (p. 166), something "worse than the simple Jewish legalism" which threatened the Galatian churches (p. 168).

Second, the system's philosophical (theosophical) character, ascetic tendencies, and angelolatry point to *a pagan element.* This was probably an incipient form of Gnosticism, a very complex system whch reached its zenith in the second century. As its name would indicate, Gnosticism (related to *gnosis,* knowledge) asserted the supremacy of knowledge. That is to say, the system taught that salvation is obtained not through faith, but through knowledge. The knowledge of which the gnostics spoke, however, was not knowledge acquired by study or the normal processes of learning. It was an occult knowledge, pervaded by the superstitions of astrology and magic. Moreover, it was an esoteric knowledge, open only to those who had been initiated into the mysteries of the gnostic system. It made much of catch words and the like which were to be used as one passed through the heavens, past the planets, on the way to God.

Another characteristic feature of Gnosticism was its belief in the inherent evil of all matter. In the gnostic system only that which is spiritual, nonmaterial, is of itself good. Whatever is material or physical is of itself bad. This belief led the Gnostics into many grave errors. One concerned the doctrine of creation. If the physical world is inherently evil, as the Gnostics averred, how could God, who is pure spirit, have made it? The Gnostics argued that He did not create this world, that He has absolutely no contact with it. God, they taught, put forth from Himself a series of emanations, each a little more distant from Him and each having a little less of deity. At the end of this series there is an emanation possessing enough of deity to make a world but being removed far enough from God that his creative activities could not compromise the perfect purity of God. The world, they argued, was the creation of this lesser power, who being so far removed from God was both ignorant of and hostile to Him. In the gnostic system, therefore, the world was not viewed as God's good creation (as is taught in Gen. 1) but as a thing in itself alien to God because it is matter and not spirit.

Another error stemming from belief in the evil of matter concerned the Gnostics' approach to the Christian life. Beginning with the assumption that the body is evil, they moved in two opposite directions. Some turned to asceticism, others to licentiousness. The ascetics felt they had to free themselves from the influence of matter (the body) by inflicting punishment on their bodies. Those who gave in to license assumed an attitude of supreme indifference to things physical and material, the idea being that only the soul is important and that therefore the body may do what it pleases. Indications of both tendencies may be found in the Colossian letter, the former being opposed in 2:20ff. and the latter in 3:5ff.

3   Again, the gnostic belief in the inherent evil of matter led to an outright denial of the real incarnation of God in Christ. The contention of the Gnostics was that deity could not be united with a human body. They explained away the incarnation in either of two ways. Some did so by denying the actual humanity of Jesus, holding that He only seemed to be human. The body of Jesus, they taught, was an illusion, a phantom, only apparently real. Others explained away the incarnation by denying the real deity of Jesus. Both of these tendencies may be alluded to in the epistle, but the main thrust of Paul's argument appears to have been directed against those who were denying the deity of Christ.

5   Third, there was *a Christian element* in the Colossian error. At its heart the system was a combination of Judaism and paganism, but it wore the mask of Christianity. It did not deny Christ, but it did dethrone Him; it gave Christ a place, but not the supreme place. This Christian front made the system all the more dangerous. Error nurtured in the bosom of the church and subtly detracting from the glory of Christ always poses a graver threat to the truth than that teaching which blatantly assails His person.

III. THE EPISTLE TO THE COLOSSIANS

The standard commentaries and books on New Testament introduction may be consulted for detailed information relative to the critical problems of Colossians. The scope of the present work permits only a brief summary of matters which are of general interest.

1. *Its authorship.* The authenticity of Colossians was once seri-

ously questioned by many, but today there is almost unanimous agreement among Biblical scholars that Colossians is, as it purports to be (1:1; 4:18), from the hand of Paul. Evidence in support of this view comes from within the epistle and from the witness of early Christian writers. Meyer, in fact, concludes that the external testimony for Colossians is "so ancient and continuous and universal . . . that from this side a well-grounded doubt cannot be raised" (quoted by Dargan, p. 3).

One strong argument for the Pauline authorship of Colossians is its relation to the epistle to Philemon. Both of these books, sent to the same town and in all likelihood conveyed by the same messenger, contain the names of Paul, Timothy, Onesimus, Archippus, Epaphras, Mark, Aristarchus, Demas, and Luke. The consensus of scholarly opinion is that Philemon is incontestably Pauline, and it is the feeling of many that the strength of its position carries over to Colossians.

2. *Its date*. Colossians was obviously written during an imprisonment of Paul (4:10, 18), but the epistle contains no indication as to the place of imprisonment. Caesarea has had its advocates, but the Caesarean hypothesis has now been largely abandoned. G. S. Duncan *(St. Paul's Ephesian Ministry)* argues for Ephesus, but this view has not gained wide acceptance. One of the chief arguments against Duncan's position is that there is no certain evidence that Paul was ever a prisoner in Ephesus. Moreover, though Luke was with Paul when Colossians was written (4:14), he was not present with the apostle during the Ephesian ministry (note the absence of "we"/"us" in the Acts narrative). The traditional theory, and the one still most generally held, is that Paul was in Rome when Colossians was written. The epistle should therefore be dated about A.D. 62 or 63, during Paul's first Roman imprisonment. Perhaps it was written before Ephesians, but surely not much time separated the two epistles.

3. *Its occasion and purpose*. The immediate *occasion* for the writing of Colossians was the arrival of Epaphras in Rome with disturbing news about the presence of heresy at Colossae. However, Paul's contact with Onesimus, the runaway slave whose master lived in Colossae, may have increased his interest in the Colossian church at this time.

Paul's *purpose* in writing Colossians was threefold: (1) to express his personal interest in the Colossians, (2) to warn them against reverting to their old pagan vices (cf. 3:5ff.), and (3) to refute the false teaching which was threatening the Colossian church (see above). The last named was doubtless Paul's major concern in writing this letter.

4. *Its theme.* Each of Paul's epistles has some salient thought. For example, in Romans and Galatians the central theme is justification by faith; in Ephesians, the unity of the church as the body of Christ; in Philippians, the joy of Christian living; in Thessalonians, the doctrine of last things. Colossians proclaims the absolute supremacy and sole sufficiency of Jesus Christ. Robertson calls it Paul's "full-length portrait of Christ" (p. 12).

5. *Its relation to Ephesians.* Colossians and Ephesians, companion epistles, are remarkably alike. They are alike, for instance, in historical background. Both epistles were written by Paul out of an experience of imprisonment. Both were sent originally to believers in Asia. Both were entrusted to Tychicus, the messenger who was to bear them to their respective destinations (cf. Col. 4:7; Eph. 6:21). Moreover, many of the topics treated are common to both (the person of Christ, the church as Christ's body, ethical duties, relationships within the family, etc.). Even the language of the two epistles is strikingly similar. Moulton points out that in Colossians the margin of the English Revised Version has 72 references to Ephesians, but only 88 to all of the other Pauline epistles. Ephesians seems to be an expansion by Paul of ideas presented in compact form in Colossians.

There are also significant differences between the epistles. There is, for instance, a difference in emphasis. Both epistles are concerned with the Lordship of Christ and the unity of His body, the church. However, in Ephesians the stress is on the *church* as the body of Christ; in Colossians the emphasis is on *Christ* as the head of the church. There is also a difference of style. Colossians is terse and abrupt; Ephesians is diffuse and flowing. Colossians is specific, concrete, and elliptical; Ephesians is abstract, didactic, and general. Finally, there is a difference of mood. Colossians, argumentative and polemical, is a "letter of discussion"; Ephesians, calm and meditative, is a "letter of reflection."

FOR FURTHER STUDY

1. Read articles in a Bible dictionary on "Colossae," "Colossians," "Laodicea," "Hierapolis," "Asia," "Gnosticism," and the Roman imprisonment of Paul. *The Zondervan Pictorial Bible Dictionary* and *The New Bible Dictionary* (Eerdmans) are both useful one-volume works.
2. Find Colossae, Laodicea, Hierapolis, and Ephesus on a map of the Bible world. Position these cities in relation to today's world. An excel-

lent map to help at this point is available from the National Geographic Society, entitled "Lands of the Bible Today."

3. Read Colossians in a modern translation. Watch for recurring words and phrases.

4. Read Ephesians and make note of words, teachings, and units which are like those found in Colossians.

5. Compare the closing verses of Colossians (4:7ff.) with the closing verses of Ephesians (6:21ff.).

CHAPTER 2

Introduction

(Colossians 1:1-14)

The first fourteen verses, which contain the address (vv. 1, 2), a prayer of thanksgiving (vv. 3-8), and a prayer of petition (vv. 9-14), served originally to prepare the readers for a favorable reception of the message which follows. For us, however, these verses do more. They give us a window through which we can look in on the Colossian church and become acquainted with those who composed its membership. Here we learn, among other things, of their geographical location, of their conversion to Christ, of their progress in the Christian life, and of Paul's interest in them.

I. THE ADDRESS (1:1, 2).

Verses 1 and 2 follow the standard greeting-form of first-century letters ("X to Y, Greeting"), but Paul puts into the traditional form a distinctly Christian content. He names himself, with appropriate Christian expressions, as the author of the epistle (v. 1); identifies the readers to whom the epistle was sent, again using the language of faith (v. 2a); and then expresses the usual Pauline greeting of grace and peace (v. 2b).

1. *The writer* (v. 1). The various ways in which Paul designates himself in his epistles are of considerable interest to Bible students. In 1 and 2 Thessalonians, perhaps his earliest letters, he simply uses the name, "Paul." In his other letters he calls himself either a "prisoner," a "servant," an "apostle," or both a "servant" and an "apostle." In the present epistle he speaks of himself as *Paul, an apostle of Jesus Christ by the will of God* (v. 1a). In these words, two things are affirmed. First, the writer is an "apostle." This was his authority for writing. The literal meaning of the word is "one sent"; but at its deepest level it denoted an authorized spokesman — "one clothed with the authority and endued with the power of the sender" (Geldenhuys, *Supreme Authority*, p. 63). Such is the meaning of the word when applied to the Twelve (e.g., Luke

17

6:13), to Barnabas (Acts 14:14), and to Paul. The word is occasionally used in the New Testament in the weakened sense of "messenger" (e.g., John 13:16; 2 Cor. 8:23; Phil. 2:25). Adronicus and Junias (Rom. 16:7) were probably "apostles" in this sense. In the passage under consideration, however, the term is used in its fullest and deepest sense to designate Paul as a commissioned ambassador for Christ. Paul seems to have insisted on his apostleship in this letter not because his authority was being attacked and denied (as in the Galatian churches) but because he was not personally known by the Colossians (cf. Romans).

Second, the writer is an apostle "by [through] the will of God." That is to say, he was not a self-appointed apostle nor was he appointed by men; he was put into the office by an act of God. In Romans 1:1 Paul speaks of being "called" to be an apostle. The First Epistle to Timothy affirms that his apostleship was "by command of God" (1:1, RSV). Galatians stresses the fact that Paul's apostleship was "not from men nor through man, but through Jesus Christ and God the Father" (1:1, RSV). The mention of the divine will, found in the present passage, occurs also in 1 Corinthians 1:1; 2 Corinthians 1:1; Ephesians 1:1; and 2 Timothy 1:1. Maclaren says the words are "at once an assertion of Divine authority, a declaration of independence of all human teaching or appointment, and a most lowly disclaimer of individual merit or personal power" (p. 9).

Timothy, who is here identified as a "brother" (i.e., fellow Christian) of Paul, was named merely as a matter of courtesy. He appears to have had no part in the actual writing of the book (cf. 4:18). (It is true that the first person plural pronoun is occasionally used [1:3, 4, 9], but ordinarily the singular form is found [1:24, 25, 29; 2:1-5; 4:7-18].) Timothy was with Paul at the time the epistle was written and apparently was known by the Colossian Christians. Paul therefore thought it appropriate to include his name in the opening greeting.

2. *The readers* (v. 2a). The Colossian Christians are not addressed as a "church" but as *the saints and faithful brethren in Christ which are at Colosse* (v. 2a). From this designation we may delineate a fourfold description of the recipients of this letter. First, they are "saints." This word, which literally means "holy ones" or "dedicated persons" (i.e., persons set apart by and for God), marks the Colossian Christians as the people of God (cf. NEB, TCNT, TEV). In Old Testament times the Israelites, as a people set apart, were God's saints (cf. 2 Chron. 6:41; Ps. 30:4, et al.). Now it is believers in Jesus who are saints, that is, the people of

God (cf. 1 Pet. 2:9, 10). C. F. D. Moule interprets the term in the present passage to mean "God's own" (p. 45).

The main idea in the word is not excellence of character but separation to God. Accordingly, in the Old Testament holiness is ascribed not only to persons (Lev. 20:7; Deut. 7:6; 2 Kings 4:9, et al.), but also to places (Exod. 29:31; Lev. 6:16, 26; Deut. 23:14; Ps. 65:4, et al.), things (Exod. 28:2; 29:6; 30:25; Num. 5:17, et al.), seasons (Exod. 31:14, et al.), etc. In such references the word "holy" only affirms that the things so described were set apart for God's purposes and service. In the same way, Christians, as saints (i.e., holy people), are consecrated to the service and worship of God. It is right to expect that such consecration will lead to practical holiness of life, but we must sadly admit that moral failures often mark the people of God (cf. 1 Corinthians).

Second, the readers are "faithful brethren." Most interpreters think the word "faithful" should be interpreted in the sense of believing (cf. Weymouth, Montgomery, NEB); however, there may also be in it the secondary sense of loyalty to Christ (cf. TCNT). Goodspeed translates it "steadfast."

"Brethren," a term of affection, calls attention to the intimacy of the fellowship of the Christian community. Despite their differences of culture, social status, and racial background, they were bound together by a common bond of love and constituted one spiritual family. But there is more. The word points not merely to intimacy of fellowship but to oneness of parentage. Christians are brothers because they are begotten of one Father. The term, then, "leads straight to the doctrine of regeneration" (Maclaren, p. 15).[1]

Third, the readers are "in Christ." This phrase, used by Paul at least 164 times in various forms ("in the Lord," "in him," "in whom," etc.), points up the spiritual position of believers. They are in Christ in the sense that they are united with Christ, joined to Him as closely as limbs are joined to the body of which they are a part. The NEB renders it "incorporate in Christ." Williams has "faithful brothers... who are in union with Christ." It is by

---

[1] Our discussion of "saints and faithful brethren" has assumed the correctness of this rendering. It should be pointed out, however, that the Greek word rendered "saints" may be taken as an attributive adjective modifying "brethren." Mrs. Montgomery, for instance, renders the whole phrase, "the holy and believing brothers." Moffatt and Williams have "the consecrated and faithful brothers." Goodspeed's translation is similar. If the traditional rendering is followed, we must be careful not to interpret it as drawing a distinction between "saints" and "faithful brethren." The latter words must be thought of as a sort of supplementary explanation. The meaning then is, "the saints; that is, the faithful brethren in Christ" (cf. Lightfoot, p. 132; Eadie, p. 3).

virtue of this union with Christ that Christians are both saints and brothers. Scott reminds us that "the name 'Christian' was still a somewhat contemptuous one, applied to the believers by the heathen. Paul avoids it, and yet conveys its meaning by his term 'in Christ' " (p. 14).

Fourth, the readers are "at Colossae." This was a river town located about 100 miles east of Ephesus in the Roman province of Asia (modern Turkey). In an earlier period Colossae had been a rather large and important city. In Paul's day, however, it was "small and obscure," a place which "hovered between town and village, a townlet" (H. C. G. Moule, p. 18). Lightfoot called the Colossian church "the least important church to which any epistle of St. Paul was addressed" (p. 16).

There is no record in the Book of Acts of Paul's work in this city. Likely it was evangelized by Epaphras during the apostle's three-year stay in Ephesus (cf. Acts 19:10; Col. 1:7).

3. *The Christian greeting* (v. 2b). The greeting takes the form of a prayer for *grace* and *peace* to be given to the readers. This combination of terms, found precisely in this form in all the epistles of Paul except those to Timothy, reflects the Greek and Hebrew greetings, respectively. The Greek word for "grace," which denotes the favor of God, is related to the word for "joy." Basically then grace may be thought of as that which causes joy. Moulton defines it as "the free and undeserved giving by God to men what they cannot achieve themselves" (p. 81). Nicholson calls it the "well-spring of all mercies to sinners" (p. 25). Williams translates it "spiritual blessing."

"Peace," a term occurring more than 100 times in the New Testament, is (like "grace") a part of Paul's greeting in every letter. In our thinking the word usually suggests the absence of conflict, but in the New Testament the concept is much richer and broader. Daille speaks of it as "the calm tranquility of a soul that looks to the Lord with confidence" (p. 16). Among the Jews the word denoted wholeness or soundness, and something of this is brought over into the New Testament. In passages such as the present one, spiritual prosperity is perhaps the leading thought.

Several commentaries make reference to the words of Jesus spoken on the night of His arrest: "Peace is my parting gift to you, my own peace, such as the world cannot give" (John 14:27, NEB).

II. THE PRAYER OF THANKSGIVING (1:3-8).

Letter writers in ancient times customarily inserted near the beginning of their letters a somewhat stereotyped sentence containing a few words of thanksgiving for the good health of the person addressed. Paul, while following the general custom, avoids all that is strictly formal and stereotyped. In his writings the conventional thanksgiving is transformed into "a heartfelt expression of gratitude for the goodness God has manifested to his people" (Beare, p. 149). The apostle's thanksgivings are therefore warm and personal and are framed in such a way that they lead up naturally to the main theme to be discussed. At the same time they are the means of establishing a bond of understanding and confidence between him and his readers. Any hostility which subsequent rebukes and criticisms might provoke is disarmed in advance by his sincere expressions of interest and praise. Often Paul's thanksgivings contain words and phrases which give an intimation of concepts to be developed more fully in the body of the letter. (Observe in the present passage the references to "the word of the truth" [v. 5, rsv], "the grace of God" [v. 6], etc.)

Appeals for thanksgiving run through Colossians like the refrain of a song (cf. 1:12; 2:7; 3:15, 17; 4:2). The present passage, which expresses the apostle's own gratitude, shows that what he enjoined upon others, he himself practiced.

The content of the thanksgiving is determined by the condition of the church, and by Paul's relation to it through Epaphras. In it we may observe (1) the circumstances and character of the apostle's thanksgiving (v. 3) and (2) the grounds and occasion for it (vv. 4-8).

1. *Its circumstances and character* (v. 3). Paul addresses his thanksgiving to *God,* thus recognizing that He is the one responsible for the virtues and graces of His people and for the ultimate success of the Gospel — both of which items are mentioned in the verses which follow.

God is identified as *the Father of our Lord Jesus Christ.* The Greek manuscripts exhibit considerable variety at this point. Some read "God and the Father of ..." (cf. KJV); some, "the God and Father of ..." (cf. Moffatt); others, "God, the Father of ..." (cf. RSV). Each of these readings yields an acceptable sense, but perhaps it is best to follow the RSV. At any rate, the suggestion in all of them is that the God to whom we pray is the God whom Jesus Christ made known to us in His character as Father. We know Him as "our Father" (v. 2) only because He has revealed Himself to us as the Father of our Lord. Daille comments that "if we have the honour to be God's children, it is by Jesus Christ, of whom he is properly the Father, having not adopted him, as he has us, but begotten him from all eternity, of his own substance" (p. 18).

Perhaps the word *always* should be construed with *we give thanks*. The thought then is, "We always thank God . . . when we pray for you" (RSV). Understood in this manner, the words affirm that thanksgiving for the Colossians was a constantly recurring thing in Paul's prayer life. The TCNT reads: "Whenever we pray, we never fail to thank God. . . ." Nicholson, commenting on the conjunction of prayer and thankfulness, calls these two things "the elements of Christian power in the world" (p. 31).

2. *Its grounds and occasion* (vv. 4-8). In expressing his gratitude, the apostle mentions specifically three things: (1) the welfare of the Colossians (vv. 4, 5), (2) the progress of the Gospel (vv. 5, 6, and (3) the work of Epaphras (vv. 7, 8).

(1) *The welfare of the Colossians* (vv. 4, 5). The first item in Paul's expression of gratitude concerns the good report which had come to him of the well-being of the Colossian Christians. He speaks of *having heard of* their *faith in Christ Jesus,* their *love . . . toward all the saints* and *the hope which is laid up* for them in the heavens (vv. 4, 5, ASV). "Having heard" translates a participle which has causal force. The meaning is "We give thanks . . . because we have heard" (Weymouth; cf. RSV). The reference to "hearing" of their spiritual condition is in keeping with the fact that Paul had not personally visited Colossae (cf. 1:9; 2:1). The source of this information was probably Epaphras (cf. v. 7).

The triad of "faith" (4a), "love" (4b), and "hope" (5a) appears with some degree of frequency in Paul's writings (e.g., Rom. 5:2-5; 1 Cor. 13:13; 1 Thess. 1:3; 5:8). "Faith," which is commitment to, or trust in, another person, is here defined as being "in Jesus Christ." This English phrase sometimes translates a Greek construction (*eis* with an accusative) which denotes Christ as the object on whom faith rests or toward whom it is directed. In this passage the Greek is different (*en* with a locative). Lightfoot (p. 133) thinks it points to Christ as the sphere in which faith operates. H. C. G. Moule, following Lightfoot, understands the phrase to speak of the Colossians' faith as "anchored in Him; resting in Him." Then he adds: "It gives us the thought of reliance going forth to Christ, and reposing on Christ, so as to sink as it were into Him, and find fixture in Him; as the anchor sinks *to* the floor of the sea, and then *into* it, that it may be held *in* it" (p. 37). Ellicott calls it "Christ-centered faith" (p. 113). Others interpret "in Christ Jesus" in terms of the Colossians' union with Christ. Moulton's rendering brings out this idea: "having heard of your faith, which you possess as people who are in Christ" (p. 10; cf. NEB).

"Love" is the fruit of faith and the proof of its genuineness (cf. Gal. 5:6; James 2:14ff.; 1 John 3:14). The Greek word denotes caring love, the love which counts no sacrifice too great for the one loved. (The verb built on the same root is used in John 3:16.) The Colossians' love is described as being "toward all the saints" (ASV). That is, it was for all the people of God (cf. TCNT). Such love bespoke the warmth of their fellowship and the depth and breadth of their brotherly concern. Perhaps the apostle was contrasting the broad goodwill of the Colossians with the narrow exclusiveness of the Gnostic heretics.

"Hope"[2] may be either subjective or objective, depending on the context in which the word is found. In the former sense it indicates the emotion or the faculty of hope (e.g., Rom. 5:2; 1 Cor. 13:13) and suggests joyful expectancy, a sense of certainty and confidence. In its objective sense, which is its use in the present passage, "hope" denotes the thing hoped for (cf. Rom. 8:24; Gal. 5:5; 1 Pet. 1:3). The reference then is to the glorious reward, that is, the future heavenly blessedness, of the people of God.

Two things are affirmed of the hope of the Colossians. First, it is *laid up* for them in the heavens. The Greek term means "stored up," like a treasure. From this assertion we may learn (1) that the object of our hope "is still in the future; (2) that its full nature is still hidden; (3) that it is absolutely secure" (Scott, p. 15).

Second, the Colossians' knowledge of hope came from the Gospel: *Long ago you heard of this hope through the message of the good news* (v. 5b, Williams). "The word of the truth of the gospel" (KJV) is a very literal rendering of the Greek. The main idea is that truth is the very essence of the Gospel (cf. RSV). The reference is to the original proclamation of the Gospel message

---

2 It is a question whether "because of the hope," etc. is to be construed with "we give thanks" (v. 3), with "your faith ... and ... love" (v. 4), or only with "love" (v. 4). In the first construction hope is thought of as expressing a reason for Paul's gratitude. This is the interpretation found, with some variation, in Moffatt, Montgomery, and Goodspeed. In the second construction hope is interpreted as a ground for, or incentive to, faith and love. Or as H. C. G. Moule puts it, "a grand *occasion* to develop them, and call them out into action" (p. 41). This is the interpretation expressed in NEB. The third construction, which is only slightly different from the second, is reflected in Weymouth. Grammatically, one can make a case for any one of these, but our preference is for the first. Whatever construction one decides for, however, the position taken in our interpretation is valid, namely that hope makes up a part of the total experience of the Colossians for which Paul expresses gratitude to God.

which resulted in the Colossians' conversion. That message, preached by Epaphras, seems to be contrasted tacitly with the more recent and heretical preaching of the Gnostics (cf. Good-speed, "the true message of the gospel"; NEB, "the message of the true Gospel").

(2) *The progress of the Gospel* (vv. 5b, 6). Having mentioned the Gospel as the source from which the Colossians had heard of the Christian hope, Paul now is led to develop the thought of the Gospel's progress in the world. This is brought out in such a fashion as to suggest that this, as well as the report of the Colossians' welfare, was for Paul a basis for thankfulness.

In verse 5b Paul spoke of the Gospel as "the word of the truth" and as the instrument by which the knowledge of their heavenly hope had come to them. Now he adds two additional ideas. One is that the Gospel is a fruit-bearing power wherever it is preached. *For it has reached you [the Colossians], and remains with you, just as it has also spread through the whole world, yielding fruit there and increasing* (v. 6a, Weymouth). The import of this statement is that the truth of the Gospel is "authenticated by its ever-widening area and deepening influence on its adherents" (Peake, p. 497).

"In all the world" is not to be taken in strict literalness, as if Paul were saying that the Gospel had been preached in every place. Moulton calls it "a deliberate exaggeration" but adds that the Gospel had spread amazingly in the years between Pentecost and the time when Paul wrote this epistle (p. 10). Robertson thinks Paul had in mind "the Roman world" (p. 29).

"Bearing fruit" (ASV), which translates a dynamic (intensive) middle voice, probably points to "the inward energy of the gospel ... in its adherents" (Peake, p. 498). Lightfoot sees in it the suggestion that "the Gospel is essentially a reproductive organism, a plant whose seed is in itself" (p. 135). The term is interpreted by TEV in the very general sense of "bringing blessings." "Increasing" may be a reference to the growing number of converts in those areas where the Gospel was known. But more likely it denotes the general idea of the rapid spread of the Gospel (Peake, Lightfoot, NEB, TEV). Thus the two terms — "bearing fruit" and "increasing" — speak respectively of the inner working and the outward extension of the Gospel. Nicholson, commenting upon this, remarks that the Gospel "is not like corn, which having borne fruit, dies, even to its roots, but like a tree, which bears fruit and at the same time continues to grow" (p. 35). "The external growth," says Lightfoot, "keeps pace with the reproductive energy" (p. 135). The tense of both verbs is present, suggesting constant fruit-bearing and growth.

Since the day ye heard of it (v. 6b) shows that the growth and power of the Gospel among the Colossians had been continuous from the very beginning (cf. Weymouth).

The second assertion here made about the Gospel is that it conveys the knowledge of the grace of God. In hearing it the Colossians had come to know *the grace of God in truth* (v. 6b).[3] The grace of God is the favor of God, His "loving-kindness" (TCNT) shown to undeserving sinners. The Greek word rendered "knew" is a compound form having intensive force. Lightfoot understands it to mean "fully apprehended" (cf. RSV); Rotherham sees in it the thought of coming to know "personally." Abbott thinks it implies "active conscious recognition" (p. 199; cf. TCNT).

To know the grace of God "in truth" is to know it as it truly (really) is (cf. Moffatt, TCNT). There is an obvious allusion to the travesty of the Gospel which had been recently introduced to the Colossians by the heretical teachers. Their so-called "gospel" was not a gospel of divine grace; it was a system of rigorous prohibitions and human traditions.

(3) *The work of Epaphras* (vv. 7, 8). A third item in Paul's expression of thankfulness is the work of Epaphras, through whom the Colossians had been instructed in the Gospel. We know very little about this man. Outside of the references in this passage (vv. 4, 7, 9) his name appears only in Colossians 4:12, 13 and Philemon 23. In the former passage we learn that he was a native of Colossae and that he had ministered not only in that city but in Laodicea and Hierapolis as well. In Philemon he is described by Paul as his "fellow-prisoner in the cause of Christ Jesus" (Williams).

The name, a shortened form of Epaphroditus, is related to the word Aphrodite, which among other things denoted charm and loveliness. Moulton suggests that the English equivalent of "Epaphras" is "Mr. Handsome" (p. 11).

A man named Epaphroditus is mentioned in Philippians 2:25 and 4:18, but he is not to be identified with the Epaphras of our

[3] Some interpreters (e.g., Lightfoot and Abbott) construe "the grace of God" to be the object of both "heard" and "knew" (cf. ASV, RSV, TCNT). Others (e.g., Alford, Eadie, and Peake) think it is simpler and better to understand the object of the first verb to be the gospel and the latter verb alone to govern "the grace of God" (cf. KJV, Weymouth). Our interpretation reflects this latter construction.

letter. The former was a resident of the province of Macedonia; Epaphras was a resident of the province of Asia.

Three things are told us in this passage about Epaphras. First, he was Paul's *beloved fellow-servant* (7a, ASV). This means that he was, like Paul, a bondslave of Jesus Christ and that Paul looked upon him as a valued comrade in the work. The apostle delighted in associating his helpers with himself, as is indicated by the salutations of his letters and by the occurrence in these letters of terms like "fellow-servant" and "fellow-prisoner."

Second, he was *a faithful minister of Christ on our [Paul's] behalf* (v. 7b, ASV).[4] The thought seems to be that Epaphras had represented Paul, that is, had preached *in his stead,* in establishing the work at Colossae (cf. TCNT). There is perhaps the suggestion that Epaphras was himself a convert of Paul (during the Ephesian ministry?) and that Paul had delegated him to take the Gospel to the Colossians.

Peake thinks Epaphras' work was on Paul's behalf in the sense that he had accomplished a task which belonged to Paul's sphere as the Apostle of the Gentiles (p. 498). These words then are Paul's acknowledgment of his debt to Epaphras for doing a work which would naturally have devolved upon him during his mission at Ephesus. The Greek word for "minister," rendered "deacon" in Philippians 1:1 and 1 Timothy 3:8, is used here simply in the sense of "one who serves." The NEB translates it "a trusted worker."

Third, as a messenger from Colossae, Epaphras had communicated the fact of the Colossians' love: *Who also declared unto us your love in the Spirit* (v. 8, ASV). The reference may be to the love which they had for all the people of God (Peake, Scott, TCNT; cf. v. 4) or to the love which they had for Paul (Montgomery). The term itself renders *agape,* the distinctively Christian word for caring love. Calvin, who seems to find no reference to the Holy Spirit here, takes "love in the Spirit" (lit., "love in spirit") to mean "spiritual love" in contrast to "carnal friendships." The latter, he explains, "depend on external causes." On the other hand, spiritual love "has no view to the world, but is consecrated to the service of piety, and has, as it were, an internal root" (p. 141). C. F. D. Moule, who follows a similar line of interpretation, thinks the sense may be "your more than merely human love," "your spiritual, supernaturally derived love" (p. 52). Beare com-

---

[4] The KJV translates a different text: "for you," instead of "in our behalf." This is also the text preferred by Moffatt, but nearly all others are agreed that it is an inferior reading.

pares this phrase with a similar one in 2:5 ("I am with you in spirit"). It is better, however, to understand Paul's phrase to mean that it was the Spirit of God who had "inspired" (TCNT) or "awakened" (Goodspeed) this love in his readers. (Compare NEB: "God-given love.") Their love, then, was an expression of their relationship with the Spirit (cf. Gal. 5:22). (Incidentally, this is the only reference to the Holy Spirit in Colossians).

There were other matters not so favorable which Epaphras told Paul about the Colossians, but for the moment the apostle "dwells on the bright features in the report" (Scott, p. 16).

III. THE PRAYER OF PETITION (1:9-14).

To the thanksgiving of verses 3-8, the apostle adds a fervent petition (vv. 9-14). He prays that the Colossians may be so filled with the knowledge of God's will (v. 9) that they may be enabled to live worthily of the Lord, pleasing Him in everything (v. 10a). This worthy life is defined as involving fruitfulness in every good work (v. 10b), growth in (or by) the knowledge of God (v. 10c), patience and long-suffering (v. 11), and gratitude to God for the blessings of redemption (vv. 12-14).

Alexander Maclaren has said that "the freedom and heartiness of our prayers for others are a very sharp test of both our piety to God and our love to men" (p. 38). Paul's prayers show him to have been a man profoundly devoted to God and generous and loving in his relations with men.

Anyone wishing to know how and what to pray for others should consider carefully the structure and meaning of this noble prayer of Paul. We shall observe first the reason for it (v. 9a) and then the substance of it (vv. 9b-14).

1. *The reason for the prayer* (v. 9a). The reason for the prayer is suggested by the opening words of verse 9: *For this cause.* Referring back to the entire discussion of verses 3-8, they show that the petitionary prayer is Paul's response to the news which had come to him of the Colossians' experience in Christ. He was grateful for what had already happened to them. He prays now for the further enrichment of their lives.

It is not certain whether the Greek word rendered *also* should be construed with "for this cause" or with "we." C. F. D. Moule prefers the former construction and interprets it to mean "that is *precisely* why" or "that, in fact, is why" (p. 52). H. C. G. Moule, who follows the latter arrangement, interprets the "we also" to mean "we on our part, meeting your love with a love-prompted prayer" (p. 48). Either way, there is obviously a close connection with the preceding paragraph.

2. *The substance of the prayer* (vv. 9b-14). Essentially, Paul's prayer was for two things: (1) that his readers might have a knowledge of the will of God (v. 9b) and (2) that they might live a worthy Christian life (vv. 10-14). Both petitions, though treated separately here, are intimately bound up one with the other.

(1) *Knowledge of the will of God* (v. 9b). The first request, and the one around which the whole prayer centers, is that the readers might be *filled with the knowledge of his (God's) will in all spiritual wisdom and understanding* (ASV). Scott thinks that in these words the apostle "begins to touch gently on his complaint against the Colossians," namely, that with all their devotion they had failed to attain true knowledge, "mistaking windy speculations for a deeper wisdom" (p. 17).

The Greek word for "knowledge," a compound form, has engendered considerable debate. Armitage Robinson, for instance, concludes that the simple, uncompounded form *(gnosis)* is the wider word and denotes knowledge in "the fullest sense." The compounded form *(epignosis)* used here is "knowledge directed toward a particular object" *(Epistle to the Ephesians,* p. 254). Earlier scholars, on the other hand, are inclined to see the word in our text *(epignosis)* as the larger and stronger word. Meyer (quoted by Peake) defines it as "the knowledge which grasps and penetrates into the object" (p. 499). H. C. G. Moule, who interprets the term similarly, uses the expressions "developed knowledge" and "spiritual knowledge" *(Cambridge Bible,* p. 68). Lightfoot remarks that "it was used especially of the knowledge of God and of Christ as being the perfection of knowledge" (p. 138). Either interpretation yields good sense; we are inclined, however, to follow the older interpreters and to understand the word as denoting *thorough knowledge,* that is, a deep and accurate comprehension. Weymouth and Goodspeed render it "clear knowledge"; TCNT, "deeper knowledge"; NEB, "insight." Such knowledge of God's will is the foundation of all Christian character and conduct.

The "will" of God in its broadest and most inclusive sense is "the whole counsel of God as made known to us in Christ" (Findlay, p. 26). This is, for us, summed up in the Bible. In the present passage the term perhaps has special reference to "the moral aspect of God's will" (Peake, p. 499), that is, His intention for the conduct of our lives.

"Filled with" may be used only in the sense of possession (cf. TCNT) or attaining to (cf. Conybeare, "fully attain to"). Probably, however, the expression suggests that knowledge of the divine will is to pervade all our being — thoughts, affections, purposes, and plans. Nothing short of the total of what God can and will give His people satisfied Paul's inspired desire. (The reader should be alert to the unusual emphasis on "fullness" in this epistle.) The recurrence of this idea suggests that the Colossian errorists claimed to offer a "fullness" of blessing and truth not found (they said) in the preaching of Epaphras. Paul answers by stressing the true fullness which is available in Christ.

"In all spiritual wisdom and understanding" is taken by some interpreters to be a fuller explanation of "knowledge of his (God's) will" (cf. TEV). The thought then is that knowledge of the divine will consists or takes the form of spiritual wisdom and understanding. Others understand the phrase to mark the means by which we acquire knowledge of the will of God (cf. Phillips, TCNT, Williams, NEB). Scroggie explains: "We do not receive divine illumination apart from our faculties, which are the means of our apprehension, and the instruments of operation. The Spirit employs those faculties of which he has endowed us, and he expects us to use them" (p. 26). Still others interpret these words to be a kind of additional concept joined to knowledge. Norlie, for instance, translates it: "We have asked that you may be filled with the knowledge of His will and that you may have wisdom and spiritual understanding in every way." Bruce's paraphrase in *The Letters of Paul* is similar.

"Wisdom," which embraces the whole range of mental faculties, is the more general of the two terms. Lightfoot calls it "mental excellence in its highest and fullest sense" (p. 139). "Understanding," having to do with correct apprehension of particular things, is more specific. Rotherham translates it "discernment"; TCNT and Moffatt, "insight." Many interpreters, however, are of the opinion that in the present passage the two words should not be treated separately but should be looked on as expressing a single thought. The use of the two words simply gives a certain fullness to the statement and thus deepens its impression on the reader. The primary idea, then, is that of "practical wisdom, good sense, clear discernment of right and wrong" (Beare, p. 150). The adjective ("spiritual") qualifies both words (as in ASV).

(2) *A worthy life* (vv. 10-14). Paul's second petition is that the Colossians might walk worthily of the Lord (v. 10a, ASV). This petition, however, is not independent of what precedes it. It is built upon and grows out of the request of knowledge. To put

it another way, walking worthily of the Lord is represented in the text as a result (or purpose) of knowing God's will. This suggests that knowledge of God's will is not imparted as an end in itself; that is, it is not imparted to us simply to satisfy our curiosity. It is given with a practical intent, namely, that we might live a life that is pleasing to God. "The end of all knowledge, the Apostle would say, is conduct" (Lightfoot, p. 139).

The Greek verb for "walk," which often is used in Scripture for the idea of living or conducting one's life (cf. Col. 1:10; 2:6; 3:7; 4:5; Eph. 2:2; 10; 4:1, 17; 5:2, 8, 15; 1 Thess. 2:12; 1 John 1:6, 7; 2:6, etc.), denotes life in its outward expression. Moffatt renders it "lead a life." Others (e.g., TCNT) use "live."

To walk "worthily of the Lord" means in general to live a life which is commensurate with what the Lord has done for us and is to us. To state it otherwise, it is to act in conformity with our union with Christ and with His purpose for our lives. Norlie's rendering ("that your lives may be a credit to the Lord") may be a bit too strong, but something of that idea is in the text.

What it means to walk worthily of the Lord is more specifically stated in the words *unto all pleasing* (v. 10a). That is to say, we are so to conduct ourselves as to please God in every way. Moffatt has, "give him entire satisfaction"; Goodspeed, "be . . . wholly pleasing to him." Phillips paraphrases it, "bring joy to his heart."

The Greek word for "pleasing" suggests an attitude of mind which anticipates every wish. In classical Greek it had a bad connotation, denoting, as H. C. G. Moule observes,

> a cringing and subservient habit, ready to do anything to please a patron; not only to meet but to anticipate his most trivial wishes. But when transferred to . . . the believer's relations to his Lord, the word at once rises by its associations. *To do anything* to meet, to anticipate His wishes is not only the most beneficial but the most absolutely right thing we could do. It is His eternal due; it is at the same time the surest path to our own highest development and gain *(Cambridge Bible for Schools, p. 72).*

Verses 10b-14 point up some of the elements in, or constituent parts of, the kind of life that is pleasing to the Lord. The leading ideas, expressed in the Greek by four participles, are rendered in English by "bearing fruit" (v. 10b, ASV), "increasing" (v. 10c), "strengthened" (v. 11a), and "giving thanks" (v. 12). Grammatically, they all modify the word "walk."

a. *Bearing fruit* (v. 10b, ASV) translates a present tense, the meaning being that the Christian life is to exhibit *continual* fruitfulness. Williams: "perennially bearing fruit." The fruit itself consists in *every good work*. TCNT: "every kind of good action." NEB: "active goodness of every kind." This includes such things as acts of worship (prayer, praise, etc.), service done for other people (deeds of kindness, charity, etc.), and the cultivation in one's own life of such Christian virtues as meekness, longsuffering, and self-control.

Paul lays great stress on good works in his letters (cf. Eph. 2:10; Gal. 5:5; Titus 1:16; 2:7, 14; 3:8, 15, etc.). However, he represents them as the fruit, not the root, of a right relationship with God.

b. The Christian should not only bear the fruit of good works in his life; he should at the same time experience personal spiritual enlargement. This idea is expressed in the words *increasing in the knowledge of God* (v. 10c). In this translation the preposition "in" (found in ASV, RSV, NEB, TEV, and most other versions) represents the knowledge of God as the sphere or realm in which spiritual growth takes place. It is possible, however, to translate the phrase "increasing *by* the knowledge of God." When rendered in this manner, the text affirms that the knowledge of God is *the means by which* the Christian grows. What rain and sunshine are to the nurture of plants, the knowledge of God is to the growth and maturing of the spiritual life. This is the interpretation preferred by Lightfoot, Peake, and others. "Increasing," like "bearing fruit," represents a present tense and puts emphasis on continuous action. "Growing continually" expresses the meaning.

c. *Strengthened with all power* (v. 11a. ASV) suggests a third element in the life pleasing to God. We are engaged in moral conflict with the cosmic powers of a darkened world (cf. Eph. 6:12), and nothing short of divine empowerment can enable us to stand. "Strengthened," representing another present tense participle, speaks of continuous empowerment. It translates the same root word which is used in Philippians 4:13: "I can do everything in the strength of him who *makes me strong*" (TCNT). "Paul," says Moulton, "insists that the high standards of the Christian life are not meant to be lived up to by our own efforts, but by divine power" (p. 14).

This empowerment is *according to the might of his (God's) glory* (v. 11a, ASV). That is to say, it is not proportioned simply to our need, but to God's abundant supply. "According to" means according to the measure of, on the scale of. The "might of his glory" denotes the might of God's own manifested nature (cf.

Eph. 1:19).[5] The RSV and some other versions, however, interpret the phrase as the equivalent of "glorious might."

The threefold issue of such empowerment is *patience, long-suffering,* and *joy* (v. 11b, ASV; cf. NEB). "Patience," which to us connotes a rather passive virtue, translates a Greek word which has an active force about it. The opposite of cowardice and despondency, it might be best rendered by "endurance" (cf. RSV, Goodspeed, Weymouth, et al.) or "fortitude" (NEB). (Compare Mark 13:13.) Beare defines it as "the capacity to see things through" (p. 158). "Longsuffering" is the opposite of wrath or revenge. It speaks of even-temperedness. It is the attitude which does not retaliate in spite of injury or insult. (Compare the use of the word and its cognate verb in James 5:7-11.)

It is debatable whether "with joy" should be construed with "patience and suffering," with the word "strengthened," or with "giving thanks" (cf. NASB). Most commentaries, as well as most of the versions (ASV, RSV, etc.), prefer the first construction. Joy, then, is seen as the pervading element of patience and longsuffering. Goodspeed renders it "the cheerful exercise of endurance and forbearance."

d. The fourth ingredient, and the crowning virtue, of the worthy Christian life is gratitude: *Giving thanks unto the Father* (v. 12). The reference to God as "the Father" shows that the expression of thankfulness is related particularly to our filial consciousness. In all that we receive from God we recognize the bounty of a loving Father and know ourselves to be His sons.

Verses 12-14 set forth four things which God has done for us, and these especially call for our thanksgiving. First, He has *made us meet to be partakers of the inheritance of the saints in light* (v. 12, ASV). "Made us meet" means that God has "qualified us" (Moffatt, RSV; cf. 2 Cor. 3:6). Norlie: "made us fit." The Greek word, which basically has in it the thought of making sufficient or competent, may shade into the sense of empowering or authorizing. Goodspeed therefore renders it "entitled." From the use of the word in this passage we may conclude that in ourselves we have no fitness for sharing in the heritage of God's people.[6] We can

---

[5] Paul uses the word "glory" more than seventy times. Its basic meaning is physical brightness or radiance, but its exact meaning must be determined by the various contexts in which it is used. We understand it here to refer to the revealed splendor or majesty of God. Dargan calls it "the sum of divine perfections" (p. 13).

[6] The use of the word "inheritance" enforces the thought that human effort and merit have nothing to do with our privileged position. An inheritance is

experience this only as God qualifies us for such a privilege. The tense of the word is aorist, pointing to the time of the Colossians' conversion. The suggestion is that the making meet is not a progressive process but an instantaneous act. Perhaps there is such a thing as "ripening for heaven," but this concerns our capacity for enjoying, not our essential fitness for it.

To be "partakers of the inheritance of the saints" is to have a portion or a share of the heritage belonging to God's people. There is an obvious allusion to the inheritance of ancient Israel in the Land of Promise, and the share of that inheritance which each Israelite had. The new people of God (Christians) also have an inheritance, and each believer has a share allotted to him.

"In light" is understood by some interpreters as a modifier of "saints." The whole phrase then would designate those Christians who have passed on to glory. It is perhaps preferable to connect "in light" with "inheritance." Construed in this manner, "in light" marks the inheritance as future and heavenly.[7] TCNT: "the lot which awaits Christ's People in the realm of Light." Light, which suggests purity and perfection, is a fitting symbol for that realm where there is no night, and where sin cannot enter.

Second, God has *delivered us out of the power of darkness* (v. 13a, ASV). "Delivered," translating a word which means to "rescue," to "liberate," implies the miserable state out of which the Colossians had been delivered. "Darkness" in Scripture is symbolic of ignorance, falsehood, and sin (cf. John 3:19; Rom. 13:12). The "power" of darkness suggests the authority or dominion which evil exercises. Lightfoot thinks that in this context the word has the connotation of tyranny. Abbott, however, who doubts that the word can have this meaning, insists that it always has the simple sense of authority. The idea of tyranny, if it is here, comes from "darkness." Compare Luke 22:53: "This is your hour, and the power (jurisdiction) of darkness."

Third, God has *translated us into the kingdom of the Son of his love* (v. 13b, ASV). "Translated" renders a word which was used

a thing allotted to, conferred upon, a person by virtue of a relationship. We were *born into* our inheritance (1 Pet. 1:3,4).

[7] H. C. G. Moule and others would not limit the inheritance to heaven. Moule admits that at first sight this may appear to be the meaning, but he contends that closer study of the context shows that the reference is "properly to the believer's position and possession even now. This Canaan," he explains, "is not in the distance, beyond death; it is about us today, in our home, in our family, in our business, ... in all that makes up mortal life" (pp. 65, 66). (Compare Phillips' rendering.) Nicholson sees both ideas, the present and the future, in the text.

in secular literature of removing persons from one country and settling them as colonists and citizens in another country. The RSV uses "transferred"; Phillips renders it "reestablished." The tense of the verb, like those in verses 12 and 13a, points to the time of conversion. The "kingdom" (rule) is not to be interpreted eschatologically. It is for the Colossians a present reality (cf. John 3:3-5). Nor is the kingdom to be interpreted in a territorial sense. That is to say, it is not an area which may be designated on a map; it is the sovereign rule of the Lord Christ over human hearts.

"The Son of his [God's] love" is a Hebraic way of saying "his dear Son" (KJV). The RSV has "beloved Son." The phrase is reminiscent of the words of the Father at the baptism and the transfiguration of Jesus.

Fourth, in Christ God has redeemed us and forgiven us our sins (v. 14, ASV). "In whom," which has its antecedent in "the Son" (v. 13), affirms that redemption and forgiveness are ours by virtue of union with Christ. "Redemption," a term which speaks of a release brought about by the payment of a price, was used of the deliverance of slaves from bondage or of prisoners of war from captivity. C. F. D. Moule renders it "emancipation" (p. 58). Goodspeed employs the figure of ransoming. In asserting that "we have" this redemption, Paul teaches that it is a present possession.

Placed in apposition with the word "redemption" is the phrase, "the forgiveness of our sins" (v. 14b, ASV). The literal meaning of the word for "forgiveness" is "a sending away." It thus speaks of the removal of our sins from us, so that they are no longer barriers which separate us from God. Redemption and forgiveness are not exactly parallel or identical concepts, but by putting the two terms in apposition one with the other the apostle teaches that the central feature of redemption is the forgiveness of sins.

The KJV adds the words "through his blood" (v. 14). The best Greek texts, however, do not contain them, and this explains their omission from versions such as ASV and RSV. The words are genuine in Ephesians 1:7, where there is a thought very similar to the one expressed here.

For Further Study

1. Compare Colossians 1:1,2 with Ephesians 1:1,2. Compare Colossians 1:3-8 with Philippians 1:3-8.

2. Study the prayers of Paul in Colossians, Ephesians, and Philippians. Make a list of the leading requests found in each prayer and then compare the lists.

3. Consider the place which is given in your life to the will of God. How full is your knowledge of His will?

4. Using a concordance, study the use of the word "walk" in the epistles of Paul. Then consider the occurrences of the same word in the epistles of John.

5. Use a concordance to study words such as "power," "might," "strength" in the epistles of Paul.

6. Use a concordance to study the ideas of "patience," "longsuffering," "joy," "giving thanks." Note especially the prominence of the last expression in Colossians.

7. Study what is said about forgiveness in this epistle.

8. Spurgeon has nineteen sermons on Colossians in his *Treasury of the New Testament* (Zondervan). See especially "That Horrible East Wind!" (Col. 3:5), and "Method and Music, or The Art of Holy and Happy Living" (3:17).

CHAPTER 3

The Supremacy of Christ

(Colossians 1:15-23)

There were at least three perilous consequences of the Colossian heresy: (1) It perverted the doctrine of salvation by grace. This it did by teaching that faith in Christ, by itself, is inadequate to save. (2) By its insistence on asceticism or (in some instances) its encouragement to license, it misinterpreted the Christian life. But the most perilous aspect of the Colossian heresy was (3) its depreciation of the person of Jesus Christ. To the errorists of Colossae Christ was not the triumphant Redeemer to whom all authority in heaven and on earth has been committed. At best He was only one of many spirit beings who bridged the space between God and men.

The present passage is a part of Paul's answer to this heretical teaching. One of several great Christological passages in Paul (cf. Col. 2:9-15; Eph. 1:20-23; Phil. 2:5-11), it proclaims the absolute and unqualified supremacy of our Redeemer. Beare sees in it a statement of "the primal significance of Christ" (p. 162). C. F. D. Moule calls it "perhaps the most striking of all the Pauline expressions of conviction as to the status of Christ" (p. 58). H. C. G. Moule speaks of it as having "the highest possible importance for Christian Doctrine" (p. 72). Nicholson comments that "as a Christological statement, it has scarcely an equal, certainly no superior" (p. 71). Scott says it "represents a loftier conception of Christ's person than is found anywhere else in the writings of Paul" (p. 20). The affirmations of the passage are all the more remarkable when we remember that they were written of One who only thirty years earlier had died on a Roman cross.

It is somewhat arbitrary to separate this passage from that which precedes. So imperceptibly does Paul glide from prayer (vv. 3-14) to exposition that it is difficult to know exactly where one leaves off and the other begins. In KJV, for instance, everything from verse 9 through verse 18 is treated as a single sentence. The ASV places a period at the end of verse 17. The RSV, which begins a new sentence (and a new paragraph) with verse 15, seems to represent the best construction of the passage. Following this arrangement, we shall note first the scope of Christ's supremacy (vv. 15-18) and then its grounds (vv. 19-23).

I. THE SCOPE OF CHRIST'S SUPREMACY (1:15-18).

In verses 15-18 there are three profound and sweeping statements concerning Christ. These statements show His relation to deity (v. 15a), to creation (vv. 15b-17), and to the church, the new creation (v. 18). In making these assertions Paul's aim was to refute the Colossian errorists, in whose system angelic mediators usurped the place and function of Christ. His task in earlier correspondence had been to expound the importance of Christ for salvation; in the face of this new teaching at Colossae he found it necessary to affirm Christ's cosmic significance. The leading ideas of the passage are strikingly similar to those found in Hebrews 1:2-4 and John 1:1-18.

1. *Christ and Deity* (v. 15a). In relation to Deity, Christ is declared to be *the image of the invisible God* (v. 15a; cf. 2 Cor. 4:4). In interpreting the significance of this statement, at least two cautions should be expressed. The first is that we need not interpret Paul's assertion in a crassly material way. That is to say, we must not understand the apostle to be teaching that Christ is the image of God in a material or physical sense. The true meaning must be sought on a level deeper than this.

The other caution is that we not limit this concept to one stage or period of Christ's existence. Some interpreters think Paul's primary reference was to the preincarnate Christ. Others prefer to think the apostle was asserting this of Christ as incarnate and glorified. For instance, Peake says the passage assumes the pre-existence of the Son, but its assertions are of the exalted Christ (p. 502). The statements of verses 15b, 16, which speak of Christ's relation to creation, suggest the former view. On the other hand, verse 14, which immediately precedes this statement, might lend support to the latter interpretation. In view of this uncertainty, it seems best not to limit the concept at all. Christ always has been, is, and always will be the image of God. Nicholson adds that though it was not the incarnation that made Christ the image of God, it did bring Him, "as being that Image, within our grasp" (p. 75).

Two ideas are in the Greek word for "image." One is *likeness,* a thought brought out in the rendering of Moffatt, Goodspeed, Williams, and Knox.[1] Christ then is the image of God in the sense that He is like God. Indeed, He is the *exact likeness* of God, like the image on a coin or the reflection in a mirror. The statement is similar to that found in Hebrews 1:3, which declares that Christ is "the brightness of his [the Father's] glory, and the express image of his person" (KJV). *The Amplified Bible:* "the perfect imprint *and* very image of [God's] nature"; RSV, "He reflects the glory of God and bears the very stamp of his nature." Something of this is involved in Paul's statement in the present passage. Christ is image of God in the sense that He is the perfect likeness of God. "He who has seen me," Christ said, "has seen the Father" (John 14:9, RSV).

The other idea in the Greek word for "image" is *manifestation*. Phillips renders it "visible expression"; Weymouth, "visible representation." The TCNT reads: "Christ is the very incarnation of the invisible God." The thought is similar to that of John 1:18, "No man hath seen God at any time; the only begotten Son, which is in the bosom of the Father, he hath declared him," KJV; ("made him known," RSV). Christ then is the image of God in the sense that the nature and being of God are perfectly revealed in Him. He brings into view and makes knowable the God who, both to our physical eyes and to our inward eyes, is invisible. That Paul was not thinking simply of physical visibility or invisibility is suggested by the declaration of 2 Corinthians 4:6 that God has "shined in our hearts, to give the light of the knowledge of the glory of God in the face of Jesus Christ."

The statement of the present text leaves no place for the vague emanations and shadowy abstractions so prominent in the gnostic system.

2. *Christ and creation* (vv. 15b-17). In relation to the universe Christ is *the first-born of all creation* (v. 15b, RSV). Each word of this phrase must be interpreted cautiously. "Firstborn," in addition to the passage under study, is also used of Christ in Colossians 1:18, Romans 8:29, Hebrews 1:6, and Revelation 1:15. (It is used also in Luke 2:7, but in a different setting.) It may denote either *priority* in time (cf. Moffatt, Goodspeed) or *supremacy* in rank (cf. NEB). In the present passage perhaps we should see both meanings. Christ is *before* all creation in time; He is also *over* it in rank and dignity. The TCNT brings this out in translation:

[1] These may be seen in *The New Testament from 26 Translations,* published by Zondervan.

". . . First-born and Head of all creation." The major stress, however, seems to be on the idea of supremacy (cf. Peake).

Lightfoot and others see in the word an allusion to the ancient custom whereby the firstborn in a family was accorded rights and privileges not shared by the other offspring. He was his Father's representative and heir, and to him the management of the household was committed. Following this line of interpretation, we may understand the passage to teach that Christ is His Father's representative and heir and has the management of the divine household (all creation) committed to Him. He is thus Lord over all God's creation.

What has already been said about "firstborn" suggests how we must interpret "of all creation." A superficial reading of the passage might lead one to the conclusion that Christ is represented as a part of creation, as simply the first of God's created beings. Such a reading of the phrase, however, is not in keeping with the context, which in the sharpest manner distinguishes Christ from creation. Nor is this understanding of the phrase demanded by the grammar. In the Greek "creation" might be construed either as an ablative of comparison ("before creation") or as a genitive. In the latter case, it is either a genitive of reference ("with reference to creation") or an objective genitive ("over creation"). Compare NEB: "his is the primacy over all created things."

Verses 16, 17 may be seen as stating the ground for Christ's dominion over creation. Essentially, they assert that Christ is firstborn (Lord) over creation because He made it. It owes its unity, its meaning, indeed, its very existence to Him.

Three prepositional phrases define the creative activity of Christ: All things came to be *in him* (v. 16a, ASV), *through him* (v. 16b, ASV), and *unto him* (v. 16c, ASV). Creation was "in him" in the sense that it occurred within the sphere of His person and power. He was its conditioning cause, its originating center, its spiritual locality. The act of creation rested, as it were, in Him.[2]

Creation is "through" Christ in the sense that He was the mediating agent through whom it actually came into being. The preposition is frequently used of Christ's redemptive mediation between God and men (cf. Eph. 2:18; 1 Thess. 5:9, et al.), but the thought here is that the entire life of the universe is mediated

---

[2] The Greek preposition may here have in it both the idea of sphere ("in," ASV) and the idea of agency ("by," KJV), but the former is doubtless the more prominent.

from God through Christ (cf. John 1:3, 10). Creation is "unto" Christ in the sense that He is the end for which all things exist, the goal toward whom all things were intended to move. They are meant "to serve His will, to contribute to His glory.... Their whole being, willingly or unwillingly, moves ... to Him; whether, as His blissful servants, they shall be as it were His throne; or as His stricken enemies, 'His footstool'" (H. C. G. Moule, p. 78).

Beare quotes one of the Greek Fathers as saying that whereas unbelievers may "debate about the End, whether it is pleasure, or speculation, or virtue, or indifference, or whatever the philosophical schools may say, it is enough for us to say that the End is Christ" (p. 167).

Several other terms in verse 16 call for comment. *All things,* used twice in the verse, translates an expression which was sometimes used in the sense of our word "universe." It denoted the totality of things, "all things" regarded as a collective whole (cf. Weymouth; NEB). That Paul uses it in the most comprehensive sense is made quite clear by the explanatory phrase, *in the heavens and upon the earth, things visible and things invisible, whether thrones or dominions or principalities or powers* (ASV).

The references to "thrones," "dominions," "principalities," and "powers" is perhaps an allusion to the angelic hierarchy which figured so prominently in gnostic teaching. Paul's mention of these things does not, of course, mean that he recognized the existence of a hierarchy of spirit beings such as the gnostics taught. His words do suggest, however, that whatever angelic powers there may be, Christ is the One who made them and He is their Lord.

The tenses of the verbs in verse 16 are significant. *Were created* (v. 16a), an aorist, points to a particular time and views creation as a definite act. *Have been created* (v. 16, ASV), a perfect tense, emphasizes the abiding result of the act. That is, it represents creation as *a resultant state.* "Stand created" might aptly render the Greek verb.

Verse 16 has stated the essential reason for Christ's lordship over creation, namely, that He is its creator. Verse 17 is a sort of summing up of the thought of verses 15 and 16. But in addition, it rounds out and completes the statement of Christ's relation to creation. *And he is before all things, and in him all things consist* (ASV). "All things," used in the sense of the whole created order, the universe, might be rendered "all things that are." In declaring that Christ is "before" all things Paul means primarily that Christ is before all in time; however, the statement is general enough to include also the notion that He is above all in rank. The thought is similar to that of the earlier expression, "firstborn of all creation" (v. 15b).

In saying that all things "consist" (lit., "hold together") in Christ, Paul reaffirms the cosmic significance of Christ. The meaning is that Christ is both the unifying principle and the personal sustainer of all creation. He is, to use the words of Lightfoot, "the principle of cohesion" who makes the universe "a cosmos instead of a chaos" (p. 156). The thought is reminiscent of Hebrews 1:3, where it is declared that Christ upholds the universe by the word of His power. Apart from Him it would disintegrate. In Him all things "live and move, and have [their] being" (Acts 17:28).

3. *Christ and the church* (v. 18). Paul's third affirmation concerning Christ's supremacy relates to the new creation: *And he is the head of the body, the church* (v. 18a; cf. 2:19; Eph. 1:22, 23; 4:15). To be the "head" of the church is to be its "directing brain," its sovereign. In the figure there is also the suggestion that Christ is the source of the church's life, but this is not its primary significance. Christ, as head of the church, is its chief, its leader. It is He who guides and governs it. The pronoun ("he") is emphatic, the meaning being that Christ alone — Christ and no other — is head of the church.

"Church," which means "assembly" or "congregation," is best interpreted here as a term embracing all of the redeemed people of God. The mention of the church as "the body" of Christ suggests at least three things: (1) that the church is a living organism, composed of members joined vitally to one another; (2) that the church is the means by which Christ carries out His purposes and performs His work; and (3) that the union which exists between Christ and His people is most intimate and vital. Together they constitute one living unit, each, in a sense, being incomplete without the other.

The words of verse 18b give one ground of Christ's headship over the church: *who is the beginning, the firstborn from the dead*. The relative pronoun ("who") is almost equivalent to "because he is" (cf. Moffatt). The word "beginning" may be interpreted in any one of three ways: as referring to (1) supremacy in rank, (2) precedence in time, or (3) creative initiative. There is, of course, truth in each of these, but it seems best to see in Paul's word the idea of creative initiative. The meaning then is that Christ is the origin and source of the church's life, the fount of its being (cf. TCNT, NEB).

"Firstborn," which is in apposition with "beginning," defines more precisely what Paul means. This term was used earlier (v. 15) to point up Christ's relation to creation. There He was described as firstborn *over all things.* Here He is the firstborn *from the dead.* We concluded that in the former passage both precedence in time and supremacy in rank are taught. In the present passage, the idea of precedence is more prominent than is the thought of supremacy. The meaning then is that Christ is the first to come from the dead in true resurrection life (i.e., never to die again; cf. 1 Cor. 15:20). And because He was the first to be born from the dead, He possessed in Himself the new and higher life which His people, by virtue of their union with Him, now share. Thus His being firstborn from the dead is that which establishes His place as the beginning, the origin, of the church's life.

The idea of sovereignty, however, is not entirely lacking in this passage. Because Christ was the first to be born from the dead, He has the dignity and sovereignty belonging to the Firstborn. Peake, who is a proponent of this view, interprets the passage to mean that "from among the dead [Christ] has passed to His throne, where He reigns as the living Lord" (p. 507).

Verse 18c is understood by some interpreters to be a kind of summary of all that Paul has affirmed from the fifteenth verse to this point: *that in all things he [Christ] might have the preeminence.* Others, more in keeping with the grammar of the statement, rightly see it as a purpose clause. Some of these construe it with all that precedes in this passage and understand the words to mean that in all that God has ever done His intention has been to exhibit the supremacy of His Son. Others, more properly, construe the clause as expressing the purpose of the immediately preceding statement about Christ's being the beginning, the firstborn from the dead. He rose from the dead in order that His preeminence might become universal, extending both to the old creation and to the new as well. He had always been first, but by His resurrection He entered upon an even wider and more significant sovereignty (cf. Rom. 1:4).

The contrast in verbs must not be overlooked. Christ *is* first in reference to all creation (v. 17); His resurrection made it possible for him to *become* first with respect to the church (cf. Phil. 2:9-11). "What He 'is' eternally to finite existence at large, He 'becomes' actually to His new Creation in His finished and victorious sacrifice and Risen Life" (H. C. G. Moule, *Cambridge Bible,* p. 82).

Others see a different significance in the word "become." These point out that by the entrance of sin, the purpose of creation as "unto Christ" (v. 17) had been frustrated and that, so far as man was concerned, Christ's rightful preeminence had been denied Him (cf. John 1:10). It was necessary, therefore, for Him to recover it, that is, to *become* preeminent. This was accomplished by His death and resurrection (cf. Rom. 14:9).

The Greek words for "in all things" have the place of emphasis. The word for "he" is normally not expressed in Greek because it is implied in the personal ending of the verb. Here, however, it is expressed, suggesting that preeminence is the exclusive right of Christ. "He himself" or "he alone" is the idea.

"Have the preeminence" literally means "have first place"; or perhaps better still, "become first." C. F. D. Moule takes the whole phrase to mean: " 'that he might be alone supreme among all' — sole head of all things" (p. 70).

II. THE BASIS FOR CHRIST'S SUPREMACY (1:19-23).

Paul has ascribed unique supremacy to Jesus Christ. He has affirmed Him to be image of God, Lord over creation, head of the church, indeed, preeminent in all things. In verses 19-23, the apostle indicates the grounds on which he affirms such supremacy of Christ. (Observe that verse 19 begins with the word "for," suggesting that the statements to follow are presented as an explanation of, or a reason for, the affirmations of the preceding verses.)

The last phrase of verse 18 implies that Christ has unshared supremacy because God has decreed it. "It was," as Calvin says, "so arranged in the providence of God" (Calvin, p. 154). The present passage states this in different terms, but still puts it within the context of the divine will. Two things which God willed are specifically set forth, one having to do with the fullness of God in Christ (v. 19), the other with the reconciling work of Christ (vv. 20-23).

1. *The fullness of God in Christ* (v. 19). Christ is supreme because *it was the good pleasure of the Father that in him should all the fulness dwell* (v. 19, ASV). The subject of the verb translated "it was the good pleasure" is uncertain. Some (e.g., C. F. D. Moule) take it to be "Christ." Lightfoot calls this view "grammatically possible" but thinks "it confuses the theology of the passage hopelessly" (p. 159). Others construe the subject to be "fulness" (cf. Moffatt, Goodspeed, RSV, Phillips). Most interpreters, however, understand the passage as affirming an action of God

(cf. TCNT, Weymouth, ASV, etc.). The expression means then that *God* willed that in Christ all fullness should dwell.

The word for "fulness," which Scott calls "perhaps the most difficult" in the epistle (p. 25), is the focal point of much discussion. The term is found about seventeen times in the New Testament, but there are only four places in which the meaning is parallel to that of the present passage. These are Ephesians 1:23 ("the fulness of him who fills all," etc.); Ephesians 3:19 ("the fulness of God"); Ephesians 4:13 ("the fulness of Christ"), and Colossians 2:9 ("the fulness of deity," RSV). The word was perhaps in current use by the false teachers, being employed by them of the totality of divine emanations, or supernatural powers ("aeons") which they believed were in control of men's lives. Calvin understands Paul to use it of "fulness of righteousness, wisdom, power, and every blessing," explaining that "whatever God has he has conferred upon his Son" (p. 154). Peake, following Meyer, Eadie, Alford, and others, interprets "fulness" to mean "the fulness of grace, 'the whole *charismatic riches of God*'" (p. 508). (Compare John 1:14.) He understands the whole statement "as having reference to the sending of the Son in the incarnation. The Father was pleased that He should come 'with the *whole treasure of Divine grace*'" (p. 508).

Others interpret "fulness" as a reference to deity. C. F. D. Moule, for instance, explains it to mean "God in all his fulness," that is, "all that God is" (p. 70). Phillips renders it "the full nature of God." The TCNT has "the divine nature in all its fulness"; NEB, "the complete being of God"; RSV, "the fulness of deity." Lightfoot paraphrases it, "the totality of Divine powers and attributes" (p. 159). Weymouth's rendering is "the whole of the divine perfections." The similar expression found in Colossians 2:9 lends support to this view.

It is significant that Paul says "all" the fulness dwells in Christ. The gnostic heretics parcelled out deity among the many spirit beings which they thought of as filling the space between God and the world. They looked upon these powers as intermediaries and taught that any communication between God and the world had to pass through them. They probably included Christ among these supernatural powers, admitting that He was of heavenly origin and that God was in some sense present in Him. He was, however, only one aspect of the divine nature and in Himself was not sufficient for all the needs of men. Paul, in contrast, declares that deity is not distributed among a hierarchy of powers; Christ is not just one of many divine beings. He is the one mediator between God and the world, and all, not part, of the attributes and activities of God are centered in Him.

"Dwell" translates a verb which suggests permanent residence as opposed to a temporary sojourn. Lightfoot thinks Paul was refuting a Colossian notion that the divine fullness had only a transient and incidental association with Christ. In distinction from this the apostle asserts that it abides in Him permanently.

The tense of the verb is aorist, perhaps having ingressive force and meaning *"take up* lasting abode." Whether the reference to "taking up" abode marks an action belonging to eternity or to time has been debated. For instance, Findlay argues for the resurrection-ascension of Jesus as the event when the fullness came to reside in the Son. Ephesians 1:20-23 and 4:8-10 are cited as confirmation of this interpretation. H. C. G. Moule feels that the context points to a time-act, but he adds that in a very real sense the fulness *"is* eternally in the Son; it does not take up its abode in Him as if it had to begin" (p. 87). Macphail, on the other hand, thinks that the grand sweep of the passage is an argument for taking the term in its widest possible range and understanding an eternal residence of the divine fullness to be meant. This is the view to be preferred. In it the aorist tense may be interpreted as constative, serving to sum up in a single point the whole action.

2. *The reconciling work of Christ* (vv. 20-23). A second reason for ascribing universal supremacy to Christ is His work of reconciliation. The Father was pleased *through him (Christ) to reconcile all things unto himself* (v. 20a, ASV). This statement sustains a close connection with verse 19. For one thing, the Greek word for "to reconcile" (v. 20), is parallel with the word for "dwell" (v. 19), both terms being grammatically dependent on the verb rendered "it was the good pleasure" (v. 19, ASV). The Father willed that all fullness should dwell in Christ; He also willed to reconcile all things to Himself through Christ. Another factor pointing up the intimate connection of verses 19 and 20 is that the action affirmed in verse 20 is dependent upon the thought of verse 19. Only one in whom the divine fullness dwelled could accomplish reconciliation.

"Through him," an obvious reference to Christ, teaches that He is God's agent in the effecting of reconciliation.

"Reconcile," the essential meaning of which is "to change" (from enmity to friendship), suggests the effecting in man of a condition of submission to, and harmony with, God (cf. Rom.

5:10, 11; 2 Cor. 5:18-20; Eph. 2:14, 15). The Greek verb, a double compound form, probably has intensive force: to change completely, to change so as to remove all enmity. The emphatic form of the word may have been deliberately chosen by Paul to insist on the completeness of Christ's reconciliation and to exclude all thought that reconciliation by angels is needed to supplement it. Some interpreters, however, understand the force of the compound to be "to reconcile again," the suggestion being that this is the restoration of a good relationship which had been previously lost (see Lightfoot, Abbott, and Beare).

This work of reconciliation is on the widest possible scale, having to do with "all things." Nicholson remarks that the Greek might be literally rendered *"the* all things," and argues from this that Paul means "the all of such things as are appointed for reconciliation" (p. 42). Others, on surer grounds, contend that the phrase must refer to the whole universe (cf. vv. 16, 17). The following phrases appear to give support to this view, for they define "all things" specifically as *things upon the earth . . . things in the heavens* (v. 20, ASV).

Calvin limits the "things in the heavens" to angels. "Men have been reconciled to God," he explains, "because they were previously alienated from Him by sin. . . . Between God and angels the state of matters is very different, for there was *there* no revolt, no sin, and consequently no separation. It was, however, necessary that angels, also, should be made to be at peace with God, for, being creatures, they were not beyond the risk of falling, had they not been confirmed by the peace of Christ. . . . Farther, in the very obedience which they render to God, there is not such absolute perfection as to give satisfaction to God in every respect, and without the need of pardon" (p. 156). H. C. G. Moule interprets similarly but admits that reconciliation affects the angelic world "in a sense as yet known only to the Lord" (p. 88). It is perhaps better to understand the word "heavens" as an inclusive statement taking in everything not belonging to "the earth." What has been called the "starry" heavens represents the thought. "Things upon the earth . . . things in the heavens" denotes, then, everything in God's universe.

One must be careful not to interpret this in such a way as to make it contradict the clear teachings of other Scriptures. Admittedly, the statement might appear, on its surface, to indicate that eventually everything will be brought into a saving relationship with God. Such universalism, however, is contrary to those passages which affirm that apart from personal trust there is no salvation. Our Lord, in fact, spoke of the impenitent as going away into "everlasting punishment" (Matt. 25:46). Most recent interpreters, therefore, understand this statement to be a reference to the *cosmic* significance of Christ's work, the thought being similar to, but not identical with, that of Romans 8:19-22. There the apostle speaks of the whole created universe waiting "with eager expectation for God's sons to be revealed," adding that "the universe itself is to be freed from the shackles of mortality and enter upon the liberty and splendour of the children of God" (NEB). The general sense is that the disorder which has characterized creation shall be done away and divine harmony shall be restored. A reflection of the same thought may be seen in Isaiah 11:6-9. In the present passage perhaps the main idea is that all things eventually are to be *decisively subdued to God's will and made to serve His purposes.*

The means by which reconciliation is accomplished is stated in the words *having made peace through the blood of his cross* (v. 20b). "Having made peace" picks up the idea which is central in the word "reconcile." The "peace" which is made may be that between God and an alienated world; or it may be the restoration of peace *within* the world. The former is the meaning to be preferred. The context implies that the making peace is the action of the Father through the Son.

"The blood of his cross" is of course a reference to the redemptive work of Jesus on the cross. The mention of "blood" emphasizes the sacrificial aspect of Christ's death; there are also in the word overtones of the covenant relationship between God and men (cf. Exod. 24:6-8).

Verse 20 has presented the general aspect of the reconciling work of Christ ("all things," etc.). Verses 21-23 now show how this applies personally and specifically to the Colossians. Mention is made of (1) their former alienation (v. 21), (2) the means by which their reconciliation was accomplished (v. 22a), (3) the state or condition which resulted (v. 22b), and (4) the evidence of the new relationship (v. 23).

a. *The former condition of the Colossians* (v. 21). Prior to their conversion to Christianity the Colossians had been *alienated and enemies.* The former word, which literally means "transferred to another owner," speaks of their estrangement from God. A perfect passive participle in Greek, the term denotes a fixed state or condition. The latter word affirms the Colossians' hostility to

God. This hostility, Paul explains, affected their *mind* (lit., "thought," "disposition," "attitude") and was outwardly expressed by *wicked works* ("evil deeds," RSV). ("By wicked works" may be construed either with "enemies" [Moffatt] or with both "alienated" and "enemies.")

b. *The means by which the Colossians' reconciliation was accomplished is denoted in the words:* **in** *the body of his* [*Christ's*] *flesh through death* (v. 22a). The "body of his flesh" is simply a reference to Christ's fleshly (i.e., physical) body. Perhaps Paul deliberately used this rather fulsome expression to emphasize (in contradiction to the views of the heretics) the reality of Christ's body. Peake, who thinks Docetism had not yet arisen, understands Paul to be alluding to and answering "the false spiritualism" of the Colossian heretics. Asserting that reconciliation could be accomplished only by spiritual (angelic) beings, they attached little or no value to the work of Christ in a physical body. In opposition to this Paul stresses the importance of Christ's physical body. "Through death" teaches that it was through the death of that body that reconciliation was accomplished.

c. *The result of Christ's reconciling work is stated in verse 22b: to present you* [*the Colossians*] *holy and without blemish and unreprovable before him* [*God*] (ASV). Some interpreters, perhaps most, take these words as a description of a yet future presentation to God (on Judgment Day). And this is the view which this passage seems naturally to suggest. There are, however, a number of scholars (e.g., Lightfoot and Beare) who see it as a statement of what God through Christ had already done for the Colossians. In reconciling them He brought them into His presence, no longer as unhallowed, stained by sin, and bearing the burden of guilt; but "holy and without blemish and unreprovable." The reference then is to the standing effected for the believer at the time of and by the death of Christ. Perhaps there is also an allusion to the inward transformation wrought in the believer upon his reception of the saving benefits of Christ's death.

Bruce presents a view in which there is a balance between the present and the future: "The sentence of justification passed upon the believer here and now anticipates the pronouncement of the judgment day; the holiness which is progressively wrought in his life by the Spirit of God here and now is to issue in perfection of glory on the day of Christ's *parousia*" (p. 213).

"Holy" suggests consecration and dedication (see the discussion of v. 2). Nicholson comments that the reference is "not ... to *conduct,* to what is called practical sanctification, but to personal condition before God. The sinner for whom Christ died is invested, to the eye of God, with all the sacredness and the value of His substitutionary sufferings, and with all the righteousness of which these sufferings were the expression" (p. 113).

"Without blemish," which translates a technical sacrificial term, was used of animals which were without flaw and therefore worthy of being offered to God. The use of this word gives support to the view that in this statement Paul was not thinking about our personal conduct but about our position in Christ. There has never been, nor will there ever be, a Christian life that is without blemish in actual conduct. But our identification with Christ is such that His righteousness and His standing before God are ours (2 Cor. 5:21; 1 John 4:17). It is in this sense that He presents us before God "without blemish."

"Unreprovable" means unchargeable, that is, having no accusation or blame. Like the other two terms, it expresses a condition possible only because we are in Christ, covered by, and sharing in, the benefits of His death for us. Williams renders the three terms "consecrated, faultless, and blameless."

d. *The evidence that reconciliation has been effected* (v. 23). Some interpreters, especially some of those who understand the foregoing words as a description of the believers' presentation before God at Judgment, explain verse 23 as a warning against indolence and complacency. The Colossians, they understand Paul to say, will be thus presented to God only *if [they] continue in the faith, grounded and settled* (KJV), and so forth. Bruce paraphrases it, "and this aim will be realized in you, if you remain in your faith. ..." His comment is: "If the Bible teaches the final perseverance of the saints, it also teaches that the saints are those who finally persevere — in Christ. Continuance is the test of reality" (p. 213).

Those who take verse 22 to be a statement of accomplished fact, contend that the words of verse 23 are proof of a past (and continuing) experience, not a condition of what is future. "No reference," affirms Nicholson, "is here made to the future, no doubt of any kind is insinuated, no threatening danger is implied. The apostle's purpose is simply to state the absolute accomplishment of salvation in the past sufferings of Christ, and the demonstration of it which is furnished to an individual soul in the present existence of his faith" (p. 122).

It is significant for both interpretations that the condition of this verse is stated in such a way as to express the apostle's confidence in his readers. The opening words might be rendered, "Assuming that you continue" or "Seeing that you continue." "The Greek," writes Radford, "indicates not an uncertain prospect but a necessary condition and an almost certain assumption. . . . St. Paul is at once insistent and confident; they must [continue], and he is sure that they will" (p. 194).

"Continue" translates a compound verb which in the New Testament is used both literally and metaphorically. In Acts 28:12, 14, where it has a literal sense, it is used of staying at a place. Here, where it is employed metaphorically, the term is used of continuing in a state or attitude.

"Faith" may denote faith as a system or body of doctrine, but perhaps here, as usual in the New Testament, it means personal faith, that is, reliance on Christ. Instead of "the faith" (KJV, ASV, RSV), it might be read "your faith" (TCNT, NEB).

The words that follow "faith" explain what is involved in continuance in faith, namely, being *stable and steadfast, not shifting from the hope of the gospel* (RSV). "Stable" (lit., "grounded") suggests being founded securely, as on a rock. "Steadfast" (lit., "settled") depicts a steady and firm resolve. When applied to a building the first word refers to "the sure foundation," the latter to "the firmness of the structure" (Abbott, p. 227).

"Not shifting from the hope of the gospel" restates the thought in a negative way. The tense of the participle, a present, expresses a continuous process, "not constantly shifting." The TCNT has, "never abandoning."

The "hope of the gospel" is the hope proclaimed by and provided in the Gospel. In its fullest sense it is the expectation of ultimate, complete salvation which will belong to believers upon the return of their Lord. Radford thinks there may be "an implicit contrast between the certainty of the promise offered by the Gospel and the delusive promises offered by the Colossian heresy" (p. 195).

In the closing words of verse 23 three statements are made to point up the importance of remaining true to the Gospel: (1) It is the message *which you heard*. The reference is to the Gospel which had been initially preached to them by Epaphras (cf. 1:7). (There is probably a tacit contrast to the perverted gospel being proclaimed by the gnostic heretics.) This Gospel, Paul goes on to say, (2) has been *preached in all creation under heaven* ("to every creature under heaven," RSV). Its universality is a mark of its authenticity. Some feel there is an allusion to Pentecost (Acts 2:5), when so many nations of the known world of that time were represented among the hearers of Peter's sermon. Offering a different view, C. F. D. Moule suggests that the statement does not mean that the Gospel had been preached to every individual, but that it had been "heard in all the great centres of the Empire (cf. Rom. 15:19-23)" (p. 73). H. C. G. Moule, followed by Abbott, thinks the reference is not so much to the actual as to "the ideal preaching of the Gospel — the preaching as it lay planned and purposed when the Lord commanded it" (p. 98). Bruce, in a somewhat similar vein, suggests that Paul was "perhaps indulging in a prophetic prolepsis" (p. 213). Scott gives a different view: "Paul's mind is still full of the thought that the whole creation has part in the work of Christ. The gospel has brought joy not to men only but to all the distracted world" (p. 28). Obviously there is an element of hyperbole in the statement.

Paul closes with the affirmation that (3) he himself *was made a minister* of the Gospel. This is a final reason for remaining true to this Gospel. Abbott comments that Paul does not designate himself in this fashion for the purpose of magnifying his office, "but to impress on his readers that the gospel which they had heard, and which was proclaimed in all the world, was the very gospel that he preached" (p. 228). Others think Paul's reason for adding this statement was to impress upon the Colossians that he was himself a living example of, and witness to, the power of the true Gospel.

I Paul is an especially emphatic expression which may reflect Paul's sense of wonder at his being commissioned a minister. "Was made" renders a word which literally means "became." The word translated "minister" *(diakonos),* has here a general sense, not the technical meaning ("deacon") which it has in Philippians (1:1) and 1 Timothy (3:8, 10, 13). H. C. G. Moule translates it "a working servant."

Paul's reference to himself as a "minister" effects the transition to the account of his mission and ministry which follows (1:24-2:7).

For Further Study

1. Read Colossians in a translation which you have not used before. Mark every name and title given to Christ.
2. Using a concordance, study the New Testament passages which refer to "principalities," "powers," etc. Note especially the occurrences of these terms in Colossians.

3. Study the word "firstborn" in the New Testament.

4. Study the idea of "fulness" in Colossians and Ephesians.

5. Make a list of some of the things Colossians teaches about the death of Jesus.

6. Study the idea of "continuing" in faith.

CHAPTER 4

The Ministry of Paul

(Colossians 1:24-2:7)

Since the church at Colossae had never been visited by Paul, there is, not surprisingly, very little in this letter that is expressly personal. The passage now to be considered, however, is exceptional in this respect. Brought in as a sort of digression, it has a decided autobiographical character. However, even it is not so much concerned with Paul the man as with the office which he filled.

Perhaps the apostle introduced this passage to justify his seeming presumption in writing to a church which he had not founded and to which he was not personally known. On other occasions (e.g., in dealing with the churches of Galatia and Corinth) he himself had expressed resentment over the interference of strangers in his work. Moreover, he had made it his policy "not to build upon another man's foundation." Paul wanted therefore to make it plain that, though the Colossian church had not been personally founded by him, he was within his rights in addressing them. In an earlier passage (1:7) he had already reminded his readers that Epaphras was in a sense his representative in bringing the Gospel to them. Now he assures them that his commission has world-wide implications; the Colossians therefore fall within the legitimate range of his authority.

In the course of his discussion Paul mentions (1) his suffering and its bearing on the Colossians (1:24), (2) his commission to preach and its implications for them (1:25-29), and (3) his personal interest in and concern for them (2:1-5). The passage closes with (4) a direct appeal to the Colossians (2:6, 7). The teaching of this passage is somewhat parallel to Ephesians 3:1ff.

I. A MINISTRY OF SUFFERING (1:24).

The preceding section, in which Paul has set forth Christ's universal and unshared supremacy, closed with a reference to the world-wide extension of the Gospel and the assertion of Paul that he had been "made a minister" of that Gospel. He now shows that it is a ministry attended by suffering: *Now I rejoice in my sufferings for your sake, and fill up on my part that which is lacking of the afflictions of Christ in my flesh for his body's sake, which is the church* (v. 24, ASV).

This is a much-disputed verse, but the general sense of it is clear. In it the apostle teaches that the sufferings which he endured in the course of his work were in the interest of the Colossians, indeed, of the whole church, and in the knowledge of that he is able to rejoice (cf. Eph. 3:13).

The opening word of the verse ("now") is both temporal and transitional in force. In its temporal sense, the word indicates that Paul's joy and his suffering were both realities at the time of writing this letter. Peake therefore explains it to mean "in my present condition as a prisoner" (p. 514). Radford, who, like Peake, interprets the word as having only temporal significance, paraphrases the sense of the verse: "The service of the Gospel, which I entered years ago, is now impeded by a prisoner's chain; yet the imprisonment has its compensations, and at this moment I am finding a new joy in the midst of my sufferings, as I reflect upon their significance" (p. 198).

There may be a note of emphasis in the word: "just now, at this very moment." Maclaren comments: "Aye, it is easy to say fine things about patience in suffering and triumph in sorrow when we are prosperous and comfortable, but it is different when we are in the furnace. This man, with the chain on his wrist, and the iron entering into his soul, with his life in danger, and all the future uncertain, can say, 'Now, I rejoice.' This bird sings in a darkened cage" (p. 118).

In its transitional sense, "now" shows that the present paragraph is closely related to the thought of the preceding section, in which Christ's unique supremacy has been expounded. Looked at in this manner, the term is almost equivalent to a "therefore" and shows that the thought of Christ's supremacy is a factor in Paul's ability to rejoice in the midst of suffering. (Other instances of "now" with a similar meaning may be found in 1 Cor. 15:20 and Rom. 7:17.)

H. C. G. Moule's paraphrase gathers up the dual reference of the word: "Now, at this very hour, in this full, solemn view of Christ," etc. (p. 99).

Three things are said in the verse about the sufferings of Paul:

1. *They are for the sake of other people.* — The apostle describes his sufferings as "for your sake" (v. 24a) and "for his body's sake" (v. 24b). The preposition employed in both phrases means not "in place of" but "in the interest of." In the first phrase it is assumed that Paul's sufferings (his bonds and imprisonment) were incurred in the course of bringing the Gospel to the Gentiles, to which class the Colossians belonged. The sufferings, therefore, were for their sake in the sense that they shared in the benefit of the ministry which brought on those sufferings (cf. Eph. 3:13).

Paul, however, thinks of himself as suffering not just for the sake of his readers but "for his [Christ's] body's sake, which is the church." That is to say, the benefit of his sufferings extends not simply to the Colossians, nor to the Gentile portion of the church only; they in some sense have bearing upon the whole body of Christ. Indeed, the apostle's sufferings contribute even to our well-being, for had he not suffered imprisonment this letter might never have been written, and we would have been deprived of its message. Maclaren's comment is apropos: "The church owes much to the violence which has shut up confessors in dungeons. Its prison literature, beginning with this letter, and ending with *Pilgrim's Progress,* has been among its most cherished treasures" (pp. 120, 21).

2. *They are identified with the afflictions of Christ.* "I . . . fill up on my part that which is lacking of the afflictions of Christ." It is this part of the verse that has evoked the greatest amount of discussion. Many Roman Catholics, for instance, interpreting the "affliction" of Christ as Christ's redemptive sufferings, have used this verse as grounds for asserting that Christ's atonement is defective and that the sufferings of the saints are needed to supplement His work on our behalf. A sign seen in a Catholic hospital read, "Don't waste suffering; offer your suffering to Jesus for souls."

But whatever is meant by "that which is lacking of the afflictions of Christ," we may be sure that Paul did not regard the death of Jesus as lacking in efficacy (cf. Col. 2:11-15). That death was complete, once for all, and wholly adequate to meet man's need. The Roman doctrine, as Lightfoot says, can only be imported into this passage "at the cost of a contradiction to the Pauline doctrine" of the satisfaction of Christ's sacrifice (p. 167).

The interpretation of Lightfoot, H. C. G. Moule, and others is somewhat similar to the Romanist view, but it avoids the suggestion of incompleteness and inadequacy in the atonement of Christ.

That is to say, their interpretation (like that of the Romanists) takes "the afflictions of Christ" to be those endured personally by Him on earth, but (unlike the Romanist view) it insists that the reference is to Christ's ministerial afflictions, not His mediatorial redemptive sufferings.

Pointing out that the word "afflictions" is never employed elsewhere in the New Testament of the sufferings of Christ on the cross, the proponents of this view argue that there could be no deficiency in Christ's atoning death and that the idea of expiation is entirely absent from this passage. The reference, then, is to the tribulations which our Lord endured in the course of His life and ministry. This interpretation is reflected in TCNT: "... in my own person I supplement the afflictions endured by the Christ."

If this approach to the passage is followed, the general thought is that Christ did not exhaust all suffering but left some for His people. The sufferings they endure in the building up of the body of Christ are a continuation of what He endured, and in that sense they supplement or complete His afflictions. "It is a simple matter of fact," writes Lightfoot, "that the afflictions of every saint and martyr do supplement the afflictions of Christ. The Church is built up by repeated acts of self-denial in successive individuals and successive generations. They continue the work which Christ began" (p. 166).

Other interpreters (e.g., Peake), on surer grounds, point to the principle of the believer's union with Christ and understand "the afflictions" to be those endured by Christ *in Paul* (and, in principle, in all of Christ's people). The thought is that the union between Christ and His people is so intimate — He the Head, they the body — that He suffers when they suffer. His personal sufferings, it is explained, are over, but His sufferings in His people continue.

Other passages expressing similar ideas are Isaiah 63:9, which declares that "in all their affliction he was afflicted"; 2 Corinthians 1:5, which affirms that "the sufferings of Christ abound in us"; and Philippians 3:10, which speaks of "the fellowship of [Christ's] sufferings." Perhaps Paul, in writing the verse before us, would have thought of Christ's words to him on the Damascus road: "Saul, Saul, why persecutest thou me? ... I am Jesus whom thou persecutest" (Acts 9:4, 5). The exalted Christ so identified Himself with His suffering people that He could in effect say, "When you persecute them, you persecute Me."

In this view, "the afflictions of Christ in my flesh" is taken as a single idea, and "that which is lacking" is not a reference to deficiency in Christ's own redemptive sufferings but to what is yet lacking in Christ's sufferings in Paul. In his experience as a prisoner the apostle was filling up the sum or quota of suffering yet remaining for him to endure.

"I fill up," which translates an unusual double compound word, is found only here in the New Testament. The tense of the verb is present: "I am in the process of filling up."[1]

3. *They are the sphere of Paul's joy.* The sufferings Paul endured for the Gospel seem never to have been to him a source of perplexity or of sadness. "You may," writes MacPhail, "occasionally hear the clang of the Roman chain, but you never hear a groan from the brave prisoner" (p. 49). Paul's testimony is: "We glory in tribulation"; "I take pleasure in reproaches"; "most gladly therefore will I rather suffer." Here he affirms: "Now I rejoice in my sufferings for your sake."

Paul's attitude had nothing in common with those monks and ascetics of a later time who inflicted torture on themselves in the belief that this would give them merit with God. Really, Paul's joy was not in suffering as such, but in "sufferings *for your sake.*" That is to say, it was the distinctive character and circumstances of his sufferings that enabled him to find joy in the midst of them. He saw them as a necessary part of his ministry and knew that they were incurred in the line of duty.

This has been the attitude of many of Christ's martyrs over the centuries. Hugh Latimer, for example, when tied to the stake along with his friend Ridley, encouraged the latter by saying, "Be of good cheer, Master Ridley. By the grace of God we'll light a candle in England today that shall never be put out!"

II. A MINISTRY OF PREACHING (1:25-29).

A second feature of Paul's ministry was the proclamation of God's message. His statement concerning this, set forth in verses 25-29, is of great value to all who wish a better understanding of preaching. Brief though it is, it might well serve as a manual to guide those who are engaged in preaching as their life work. The thought revolves around four conceptions: (1) Paul's appointment to the office of preacher (v. 25), (2) the message which he preached (vv. 25b-28a), (3) the method he employed (v. 28b), and (4) his ultimate aim (v. 29).

---

[1] Several other interpretations of verse 24 have been proposed. These are discussed in the standard commentaries, such as those by Lightfoot, Abbott, Peake, C. F. D. Moule, etc.

1. *Paul's appointment to his work* (v. 25). The fact of Paul's appointment is stated in verse 25a: "whereof [i.e., of the church] I was made a minister" (ASV). Elsewhere the apostle speaks of himself as a minister of the Gospel (v. 23; Eph. 3:7), of God (2 Cor. 6:4), of Christ (2 Cor. 11:23), of a new covenant (2 Cor. 3:6). Here he is the church's minister, and as such is bound to toil and suffer in whatever way the church's welfare requires. Suffering then is not simply a matter of joy (v. 24) but of duty as well.

The personal pronoun "I," expressed in the Greek for emphasis, suggests that Paul was thinking of a ministry peculiar to himself. "Was made" (KJV, ASV) literally means "became" (RSV), the thought being that he became a minister of the church at the Lord's call. It was not an honor which he took to himself. Weymouth: "I have been appointed." The word for "minister," the same as that used earlier of Epaphras (1:7) and of Paul (1:23), simply means "one who serves."

Paul's appointment to his office was *according to* [*that is, on the terms of*] *the dispensation* [*arrangement, plan*] *of God* (v. 25b, KJV, ASV; cf. Rotherham). This translation, which suggests that Paul looked upon his call to the ministry as part of the divine plan for the evangelization of the world, is in keeping with the fact that the word for "dispensation" is sometimes used in Scripture for the plan by which God has ordered the course of history (cf. Eph. 1:10, RSV). But the Greek term for "dispensation," related to our words "economy" (denoting careful stewardship) and "economics," is perhaps best rendered here by the word "stewardship" (cf. Luke 16:2-4). This rendering suggests that Paul conceived of the work to which God has appointed him as both a high privilege and as a sacred trust (cf. Williams, TCNT). He was a servant of the church, but in the deepest sense he was a steward of God. Ultimately, therefore, he was accountable to God, not the church. As Maclaren put it, "He is the Church's servant indeed, but it is because he is the Lord's steward" (p. 124).

This stewardship was given to Paul *to you-ward* (v. 25a, ASV), that is, with reference to, and for the benefit of, the Colossian Christians and other Gentiles (cf. v. 24).

The purpose of the apostle's stewardship was *to fulfil the word of God* (v. 25b). The idea in the word "fulfil," as used here, is to give full development to, to give full scope to. Some understand this to refer specifically to the geographical extension of the Gospel. For example, John Eadie explains it to mean that Paul carried the word "beyond the frontiers of Judaea, lifted it above the walls of the synagogue, and held it up to the nations" (p. 95). Norlie's rendering brings out the same thought: "My task was to make the Word of God fully known" (cf. RSV). Interpreted in this manner the statement is comparable to that found in Romans 15:19, "I have fully preached [Gr., "fulfilled"] the gospel of Christ."

Beare interprets "fulfil" as meaning "to make fully effective." Paul did this, he explains, "by bringing in the full complement of those for whom it [the word of God] is destined" (p. 179).

Others (e.g., Peake) interpret Paul to mean that his special ministry was to make clear the true nature of the Gospel as a divine provision intended for all men. Scott appears to have this in mind when he explains the passage in terms of proclaiming the Gospel message "in all its fulness" (p. 32).

2. *The message preached by Paul* (vv. 25b-28a). Various expressions are used in these verses to designate Paul's message. The first is *the word of God* (AV). 25b. A general term which sums up the oral proclamation of the apostles, it is frequently used as a synonym for the Gospel (cf. 1 Cor. 14:36; 2 Cor. 2:17; 4:2; 1 Thess. 2:13, et al.). Moffatt has "God's message."

Verses 26 and 27, which are a kind of digression, define the Word of God more specifically in terms of a mystery. A word borrowed from the religious vocabulary of the day, "mystery" is used in the New Testament of a truth undiscoverable except by divine revelation (cf. 1 Cor.; 2:6ff.; 15:51). In the passage under study, Weymouth and TCNT translate it "truth." In Ephesians, a companion epistle to Colossians, it is used six times — more often than in any other book of the New Testament. In 1:9 the term is used of the mystery of God's dealing with the world; in 3:3-9, where it occurs three times, the word has special reference to the inclusion of Gentiles in the privileges and blessings of the Messianic salvation; in 5:22 it speaks of the spiritual union of Christ and His church; and in 6:19 it is practically equated with the Gospel. In Colossians the word occurs four times (1:26, 27; 2:2; 4:3). Coming from a root which means to initiate, the word in a general sense denotes a secret (cf. Goodspeed). In its various contexts in the New Testament, however, "mystery" ordinarily speaks of an *open* secret (cf. Williams); that is, it denotes something which though once a secret has now been fully revealed in the Gospel.

This mystery, Paul explains, *hath been hid from ages and from generations, but now is made manifest to his saints* (v. 26b, KJV).

The words express the two characteristics of a mystery in the New Testament: "hid from ages and generations . . . now . . . made manifest."

Some interpreters (e.g., Peake) understand "ages" to refer to the ages before the creation of the world; "generations," to the generations of human history. The whole expression is thus equivalent to a declaration that the mystery under discussion had been previously concealed from both angels and men. Scott, pointing out that in the gnostic systems the terms "ages" and "generations" were used in a technical sense of the hierarchies of supernatural powers, prefers to see a similar meaning here. Such an interpretation, he explains, is in harmony with "the cosmical sweep" of the epistle (p. 33). Others take a different approach. Williams, for instance, translates it: ". . . covered up from the people of former ages and generations." This last interpretation is perhaps the simplest and best.

To the people of God ("his saints") the truth which was once hidden is now "made manifest." Conybeare has "shown openly"; Goodspeed, "disclosed"; TCNT, "revealed." The Greek construction of which this expression is a part is grammatically irregular, involving a change from a participle ("hath been hid," first part of v. 26) to an indicative verb ("made manifest," last part of the v.). The sudden shift from participle to indicative is a reflection of "Paul's intense joy that the long silence has been broken; he is content with nothing short of a definite statement of the glorious fact" (Peake, p. 516).

Verse 27 speaks of God's wishing to make known *the riches of the glory of this mystery among the Gentiles* (KJV). The thought is that God was pleased to reveal to His people how great is the glorious character of the gospel mystery. Norlie's rendering appears to capture the essential meaning: "It is God's will that this mystery shall be fully explained to all the nations in all its riches and glory." Scott, observing that "glory" in Paul's writings "carries with it the idea of something divine," thinks the whole phrase suggests "richness in divine significance" (p. 33).

"Among (lit., "in") the Gentiles" defines the sphere in which the wealth of glory has been especially displayed. Paul seems to have been thinking of the wonder of the unfolding of the divine mystery in the conversion of pagan people and in their being drawn into the one body of Christ.

The inner content of the mystery is defined as *Christ in you* (v.

27b; cf. vv. 25, 26, where the mystery is defined as the Gospel).[2] Some scholars read "Christ *among* you," that is, among you Gentiles (cf. Lightfoot). If the words are understood in this fashion, the mystery consists in the offer of redemption to the Gentiles. They had appeared to be forever excluded from God's favor, but it had been a part of God's secret plan from the beginning that they should be included in the Messianic salvation. There is much to be said for this interpretation but the context requires that we understand the phrase as referring to an inner, subjective experience. The mystery then, long hidden but now revealed, is not the *diffusion* of the Gospel among the Gentiles but the *indwelling* of Christ in His people, whether Jews or Gentiles.

"Christ in you" is now declared to be the hope of glory. "Hope" is joyous expectation or anticipation. Perhaps the thought is that the indwelling Christ is the grounds for the expectation of glory. The "glory" is that which shall belong to the Christian at the end of the age in the heavenly state (cf. Col. 3:4; Rom. 5:2; 8:17). Goodspeed renders the whole phrase, "the promise of glorification." Scott explains it as "the certainty of salvation" (p. 34). The general truth is that Christ dwelling in the believer is the ground for hope of heavenly bliss. A kindred notion is found in Ephesians 1:13, 14, where the Spirit is designated as "the earnest of our inheritance." Beare observes that in this letter "Christ himself occupies the sphere that Paul elsewhere assigns to the Spirit" (p. 181).

In verse 25 Paul has defined his message as "the word of God." In verse 26 and 27 he has used the word "mystery." Now, in verse 28, he has the expression, *whom we proclaim*. "Whom" — the antecedent is Christ — shows that Paul conceived of his message not as a system, not as a hierarchy of spirit powers, not as a collection of rules and regulations, but as a living and glorious Person who is the fulfillment of the deepest hopes of mankind and the source of new life for all of His people.

"We" is emphatic (like "I" in vv. 23 and 25) and distinguishes Paul (and his fellow preachers) from the Colossian errorists.

"Proclaim" translates a word which suggests a solemn or public proclamation. Biblical scholars of an earlier period (Westcott, Vincent, e.g.) thought there was in it the notion of proclaiming *with authority*. Kittel, who speaks of it as belonging to "the lan-

---

[2] We are interpreting the relative "which" as having its antecedent in the word mystery. John Eadie prefers to take the antecedent to be the total idea of the wealth of the glory of the mystery.

guage of mission" (Vol. I., p. 71), asserts that the term includes the idea of "instruction, admonition and tradition" (p. 72). Radford comments that the word "denotes not the enunciation of ideas but the statement of facts" (p. 208). It perhaps has a wider significance than the more common word for "preach" *(kerusso)* in Paul's writings (cf. v. 23).

3. *The method employed by Paul* (v. 28b). Two participial phrases describe the attendant circumstances of Paul's preaching — *admonishing every man and teaching every man in all wisdom* (v. 28, ASV). "Admonishing" suggests the warning (KJV, TCNT, Williams, et al.) of non-Christians, the thought probably being that the apostle sought to awaken each of them to his need of Christ. Meyer and others observe that the word corresponds to the demand for repentance in the gospels. Used in the writings of Paul eight times, it occurs nowhere else in the New Testament.

"Teaching," which probably refers to a ministry for converts, points up the importance of instruction in the proclamation of the Word. "In all wisdom" seems to express the manner in which the teaching was done (Abbott; cf. TCNT) rather than the substance of the teaching (H. C. G. Moule, Findlay; cf. Berkeley, Phillips).

"Every man," repeated three times in verse 28 for emphasis, indicates that Paul's gospel was not marred by the narrow exclusiveness which characterized the false teachers. They believed that the way of salvation was so involved and complicated that it could be understood only by a select few who made up a sort of spiritual aristocracy. Paul, unlike the errorists, slighted no person. "Every man" was the object of his direct concern.

4. *The aim of Paul's preaching* (vv. 28c, 29). The aim of Paul's proclaiming, admonishing, and teaching was to *present every man perfect in Christ* (v. 28c). "Present" refers to the bringing into God's presence at the return of Christ (cf. 1 Thess. 2:19f.; 5:23). Only then will God's work in the believer be complete. "Every man" includes both men and women, the Greek word for "man" being the generic term. The word "perfect" suggests the attaining of the proper end and goal of one's existence. Other versions use such terms as "complete" (NAB), "full grown" (Montgomery), "mature" (Williams, RSV). The reference is to maturity in faith and character (cf. Eph. 4:13), and it is a prospect held out for "every man." Such maturity is possible "in Christ," that is, by virtue of the believer's union with Christ.

To the accomplishing of this end Paul gave himself in unstinted effort: *Whereunto I labor also, striving according to his working, which worketh in me mightily* (v. 25, ASV). "I labor" translates a word which denotes wearisome toil. Weymouth: "I exert all my strength." "Striving" renders the word of which our word "agonize" is a transliteration. A term taken from the athletic arena, it signifies intense struggle. Weymouth: "like an eager wrestler." Other versions have such expressions as "contending" (Rotherham), "wrestling" (Montgomery), "struggling" (TCNT), "struggling like an athlete" (Beck). This struggle, Paul affirms, is *according to* the *working* of God. That is to say, the struggle is carried on in the measure, not of his own natural powers, but of the supernatural power at work in him. "Working" is the rendering of a Greek term from which we get the word "energy." H. C. G. Moule translates it "active force" (p. 108). It is an energy *which worketh* (lit., energizes) the apostle *mightily*. The entire statement reflects the thought that through faith in Christ one links his life with a source of strength that enables him to rise above his natural limitations.

III. A MINISTRY OF INTERCESSION (2:1-5).

A third feature of Paul's ministry was his pastoral concern for those whom he served. The concern expressed in these verses arose from Paul's anxiety about the response of the Colossian Christians to the error being propagated by the gnostic teachers. Such an expression of concern is what we would expect from the man who wrote Philippians 3:18. Anyone who shares Paul's exalted concept of Christ (cf. Col. 1:15ff.), we may add, can never be indifferent to the inroads of error.

Verse 1 gives expression to this deep concern. *For I would have you know how greatly I strive for you, and for them at Laodicea, and for as many as have not seen my face in the flesh* (ASV). "Strive" translates a word which denotes strenuous activity (cf. "striving," 1:29). Goodspeed has, ". . . what a great fight I am putting up for you." In the present context it speaks of a deep and earnest solicitude. Knox therefore expresses the meaning to be ". . . what anxiety I feel over you." A literal rendering might be, "I would have you know *what great agony* I have for you." The powers which wrestled with Paul for the ruin of his work were real and resolute; he had therefore to "meet them, foot to foot, force to force, in Christ" (H. C. G. Moule, p. 118).

The particular struggle Paul had in mind appears to have been the struggle in prayer. At the time these words were written he could not move beyond the walls of his "hired lodging," being continuously held by the chain attaching him to the Roman soldier.

But even under these circumstances he could engage in the combat of prayer and could in this manner wrestle in behalf of his readers.

This brings before us an aspect of the prayers of Paul which we often overlook. Sometimes prayer must have been for him, as it is often for us,

> ... the burthen of a sigh,
> The falling of a tear,
> The upward glancing of an eye,
> When none but God is near.

But from the words of this passage we may conclude that the apostle's prayers at other times involved him in awesome conflict, in an intense struggle of the soul. (Compare the Gethsemane experience of our Lord.) H. C. G. Moule comments:

> Prayer, genuine and victorious, is continually offered without the least physical effort or disturbance. It is often in the deepest stillness of soul and body that it wins its longest way. But there is another side of the matter. Prayer is never meant to be indolently easy, however simple and reliant it may be. It is meant to be an infinitely important transaction between man and God. And therefore very often, when subjects and circumstances call for it, it has to be viewed as a work involving labour, persistency, conflict, if it would be prayer indeed (p. 124).

Paul's agony in prayer was *for,* that is, in behalf of, the Colossians. But it was also in behalf of those *at Laodicea, and for as many as have not seen my face in the flesh* (v. 1b, ASV). Laodicea, an important banking center in ancient times, is mentioned elsewhere in the New Testament in Colossians 4:13, 15, 16 and in Revelation 3:14. Located about twelve miles from Colossae, it (like Colossae) was probably evangelized during the time of Paul's extended ministry in Ephesus. The wording of verse 1, though capable of being interpreted otherwise, probably suggests that the Colossians and the Laodiceans were among those who had "not seen [Paul's] face in the flesh."

That Paul felt such anxiety for converts with whom he was not personally acquainted and for churches which he did not by his own direct work establish is indicative of the bigness of the man.

Paul's concern for his readers was *that their hearts may be comforted* (v. 2a). The Greek word for "comforted," which literally means "to call to one's side," sometimes signifies such ideas as comfort, encouragement, exhortation, depending on the context in which it is found. Perhaps here it conveys the thought of being strengthened for trial (Robertson) or against the onslaught of error (Abbott). Beare explains it to mean "confirmed in affectionate loyalty to Christ" (p. 184).

The means by which this strengthening takes place is expressed by the words *knit together in love* (v. 2b). The verb may suggest being "compacted, welded into genuine unity" (H. C. G. Moule, p. 126; cf. Weymouth). On the other hand, the Greek word for "knit together" is always used in the Septuagint with the sense of "instruct." In this interpretation "love" denotes the spirit in which the instruction is given (Beare). Moffatt's rendering brings out a slightly different idea: "May they learn the meaning of love."

The rendering of KJV and ASV ("knit together in love") suggests that God's revelation in Christ cannot be properly understood in isolation from the fellowship of other Christians (cf. Eph. 3:17f.). The other translation teaches that instruction in love leads to a deeper comprehension of that revelation.

Two consequences of being "knit together" (or, "instructed") are now given. One is the attaining of *all riches of the full assurance of understanding*. The meaning is that being knit together (or, instructed) in love brings an inward wealth which consists in full understanding.

The word behind "full assurance" could be rendered "true conviction." The NEB translates the whole phrase "the full wealth of conviction which understanding brings." RSV: "the riches of assured understanding."

The second issue of being "knit together" (or, "instructed") is the *knowledge of God's mystery* (v. 2c, RSV). The word for "knowledge" indicates a deep or full knowledge, perhaps a true knowledge (cf. 1:9, above). The "mystery of God" is the secret which belongs to God. As brought out above, the term is used for spiritual truth which can be known only as it is disclosed by God.

The words following "mystery of God" define it. A comparison of the versions (e.g., KJV, Moffatt, ASV, RSV) reveals that there is considerable variation not only in the wording of the Greek text, but also in the way in which the scholars understand the passage.[3] Our own preference, following Lightfoot, is to accept the shorter reading (see ASV) and to understand *Christ* to be an appositive defining the mystery. This is the interpretation preferred by most modern scholars. It is represented among the versions by ASV, TCNT, Williams and NASB.

Verse 3 describes Christ as the one *in whom are all the treasures*

---

[3] For a full discussion of the textual variants see Abbott.

of wisdom and knowledge hidden (ASV). The idea is that Christ as the One in whom are all the treasures, etc. is God's great mystery (cf. 1:29). "The mystery," writes Lightfoot, "is not 'Christ,' but 'Christ as containing in Himself all the treasures of wisdom' " (p. 173). The great truth taught is that all that is deepest in God is summed up in Christ.

The two thoughts contained in this statement are: (1) all the treasures of wisdom and knowledge are in Christ, and (2) they are in Him in hidden fashion. The false teachers claimed to have a higher knowledge than that possessed by ordinary believers. Paul, against this, argues that all wisdom and knowledge are in Christ. The term "hidden" does not mean that they are concealed, but rather are laid up or stored away as a treasure. The treasure is accessible to and available for every believer.

In verse 4 Paul expresses the reason for his anxious concern. *This I say, that no one may delude you with persuasiveness of speech* (v. 4, ASV). "This I say" is a reference to the utterances of verses 1-3. The word for "delude" suggests leading astray by false reasoning. "Persuasiveness of speech," translated as "beguiling talk" by H. C. G. Moule (p. 127), expresses something of the same idea. Moffatt renders it "plausible arguments." The term suggests the attempt to convince someone by "fast talk" or by handing him a "smooth line." Paul was obviously thinking of the attempt of the errorists to lead the Colossians away from their conviction concerning Christ.

Verse 5 points up the sincerity of Paul's interest in his readers: *For though I am absent in the flesh, yet am I with you in the spirit, joying and beholding your order, and the stedfastness of your faith in Christ* (ASV). The meaning is that though he is removed from them bodily he feels a oneness with them spiritually and rejoices to see their good order and the firmness of their faith. The word for "order" was a military term connoting the orderly array of a band of disciplined soldiers. Moffatt uses "steadiness." Eadie suggests "good order" (p. 122).

"Steadfastness" translates a word which signifies solidity and compactness. Paul, in applying it to the faith of the Colossians, points up the unyielding nature of their faith or, as Eadie puts it, "the stiffness of its adherence to its one object — Christ" (p. 123). Like the word for "order," however, "steadfastness" was a term belonging to the vocabulary of military life. It may therefore mean something like "solid front" (Lightfoot p. 176). If this is the imagery intended by Paul, he envisions the situation of the Colossians to be like that of any army under attack, and affirms that their lines were unbroken and their discipline intact.

"Faith in Christ" speaks of the Colossians' reliance upon their Lord. The very mention of this by Paul indicates his deep concern that this might continue to be the attitude of the Colossians.

IV. A MINISTRY OF EXHORTATION (2:6, 7).[4]

A final feature of Paul's ministry, exemplified but not expounded here, was exhortation. In light of the danger confronting the Colossians they are urged to do two things. These are as follows:

1. *Remain true to Christ as Lord.* — *As therefore ye received Christ Jesus the Lord, so walk in him* (v. 6, ASV). "Therefore" indicates that Paul makes his appeal in light of the foregoing discussion. "As" points up that the Colossians had received Christ in a certain manner: as the Anointed of God ("Christ"), as the historic Savior ("Jesus"), and as sovereign "Lord." Paul's appeal is that in the same manner ("so") they keep on walking (present tense) "in him." That is to say, their present and continuous conduct is to conform to the doctrine which was taught them at conversion. Taylor paraphrases it: "And now just as you have trusted Christ to save you, trust Him too for each day's problems; live in vital union with Him."

The walk in Christ is expanded in verse 7a: *rooted and builded up in him, and established in your faith* (ASV). "Rooted," translating a perfect tense, suggests a once-for-all experience, that is, a being permanently rooted. "Builded up" and "established" (Moffatt: "confirmed"), present tenses, indicate a continual process.

"In your faith" conceives of faith as the body of truth (the faith system) and looks upon this as the sphere within which the being "established" takes place. Rotherham renders it "your faith," suggesting faith in its more usual sense of trust in, reliance upon, Christ. Perhaps Taylor again captures the force of it: "Let your roots grow down in Him and draw up nourishment from Him. See that you go on growing in the Lord, and become strong and vigorous in the truth." The whole appeal was to be carried out in accordance with that which had been taught the Colossians in their initial experience: *even as ye were taught* (v. 7b).

2. *Abound in thanksgiving* (v. 7c). The second appeal is that

---

[4] Many interpreters think that the two verses comprising this section are more closely related to what follows than to that which precedes them. That is to say, they are thought of as introducing the warnings of 2:8ff rather than as closing out the section on Paul's ministry (begun at 1:24). Our arrangement reflects the paragraph division of ASV.

the readers might abound in thanksgiving.[5] *Abounding,* a favorite
word of Paul, literally means "overflowing" (like a river overflowing its banks). The tense is present, meaning that thanksgiving
is to be a continual, habitual thing on the part of believers.

Thanksgiving, which Lightfoot calls "the end of all human
conduct" (p. 177), receives great emphasis in Paul's epistles. There
may be the suggestion in the present passage that those who lack
a deep sense of gratitude to God are especially vulnerable to doubt
and spiritual delusion. H. C. G. Moule writes:

> There is a great and profoundly reasonable power in holy thanks-
> giving to bring home to the soul the reality of the Treasure for
> which the thanks are given. The heart which looks up and blesses
> God for 'His unspeakable Gift,' His own Son, 'who was delivered
> for our offenses, raised for our justification,' and glorified for our
> life in glory, will develop a holy and healthy instinct of rejection
> toward all substitutes for Him (p. 130).

[5] Our discussion is based on the text of ASV. The KJV reads "abounding
therein [i.e., in faith] with thanksgiving."

FOR FURTHER STUDY

1. Compare what is said about Paul's suffering in Colossians 1:24
with what is said in Ephesians 3:13.

2. Read Colossians through, taking note of each passage in which the
idea of joy is present. Write out in your own words the teachings of the
epistle on joy. Compare the teachings of Philippians on joy.

3. Using a concordance, study the occurrences of the word "dispensation" in Colossians and Ephesians. Do the same for the word "minister."

4. Study the uses of the word "mystery" in the epistles of Paul. Check
different translations to see how the term is rendered.

5. Read Colossians through, marking each occurrence of the word
"love."

6. Write out in your own words what is said about wisdom and
knowledge in Colossians.

7. Study the use of the word "abound" in Paul's epistles.

CHAPTER 5

The Menace of Heresy

(Colossians 2:8-23)

In an earlier section (1:15-23), where Paul expounded the supremacy of Christ's person, various allusions were made to the errorists of Colossae. Now, however, the apostle makes his most direct attack against the "Colossian heresy." Indeed, most of what we know about the heresy comes from information furnished here. The entire passage bristles with exegetical difficulties, and perhaps calls for closer attention to its wording and argument than does any other part of the epistle.

The tone of the passage is both admonitory and affirmative, but admonition is the prevailing note sounded throughout. The affirmations, which mainly concern Christ and His sufficiency (cf. vv. 9-15), form the basis on which the warnings are issued and give point and power to them. The warnings concern (1) false philosophy (vv. 8-15), (2) legalism (vv. 16, 17), (3) angel worship (vv. 18, 19), and (4) asceticism (vv. 20-23). Our discussion is built around these ideas.

I. THE WARNING AGAINST FALSE PHILOSOPHY (2:8-15).

Paul's first warning is against false philosophy, or more precisely, against being taken captive *through* a false philosophy. The warning is stated in verse 8 and is justified by the affirmations of verses 9-15.

1. *The warning stated: Take heed lest there shall be any one that maketh spoil of you through his philosophy and vain deceit* (v. 8a, ASV). "Take heed" alerts the readers to the danger. The TCNT and others have "take care"; RSV, "see to it"; NEB, "be on your guard." The singular "anyone" leads some interpreters to conclude that Paul had in mind a particular person, perhaps the leader, among the heretical teachers. The mode of the verb rendered "there shall be" (future indicative) points to a real, not simply a supposable, danger. The word translated "maketh spoil"

69

might be taken to mean "rob" (cf. KJV, "spoil"; Knox, "cheat"),
but perhaps it is better to interpret it in the sense of "kidnap." A
graphic and vigorous word, it was used by one ancient Greek
writer of the abduction of a virgin. More frequently, however, it
was used of taking captives in war and leading them away as booty.
Here it depicts the false teachers as men-stealers wishing to entrap
the Colossians and drag them away into spiritual enslavement.
Weymouth: "Take care lest there be any one who leads you away
as prisoners" (cf. NEB).

The means by which the errorists attempted to do this is conveyed
in the words, "through his philosophy and vain deceit." In the
ancient world the word "philosophy" was applied to anything that
had to do with theories about God, the world, and the meaning of
life. This is the only occurrence of the word in the New Testament,
but it would be a mistake to conclude that Paul intended his statement to be a condemnation of all philosophy. The term itself is a
noble one, literally meaning "love of wisdom." In the present passage Paul, by using only one article and one preposition with the
expression "philosophy and vain deceit," intended his readers to
understand the second term ("vain deceit") as explanatory of the
first ("philosophy"). That is to say, the so-called "philosophy" of
the Colossian heretics is more aptly and precisely described as "vain
deceit" or an empty delusion. TCNT: "a hollow sham"; Phillips:
"high-sounding nonsense."

Moffatt, avoiding the use of the word philosophy, renders the
phrase "a theosophy which is specious make-believe." Doubtless
Paul's reference is to the theosophic speculations characteristic of
Gnosticism. Such speculations, he was convinced, were devoid of
all good and unable to meet the needs of the soul.

Three other descriptive phrases are used to characterize this system, and each of these constitutes a reason for its rejection. First,
it was *after [according to] the tradition of men* (v. 8b). By "tradition" Paul may mean the mass of oral tradition which the Jews
had engrafted on the written law. It is more likely, however, that
the term is a reference to various pagan theories current in that
day. The apostle's assertion is that these, not divine revelation, were
the bases of the "philosophy" of the Colossian errorists.

Second, it was a philosophy *after [according to] the rudiments
of the world* (v. 8c). "Rudiments" translates a word of multiple
meanings. Originally it denoted the letters of the alphabet, its root
meaning being "things in a row." The term then came to be used
of the elements ("ABC's") of learning (cf. Gal. 4:3, TCNT, Norlie;

Heb. 5:12, ASV, TCNT), of the physical elements of the world (cf. 2 Pet. 3:10), of the stars and other heavenly bodies (cf. 2 Pet. 3:10, Moffatt), and of the elemental spirits, that is, the supernatural powers believed by many ancients to preside over and direct the heavenly bodies (cf. Gal. 4:3, NEB).

The sense in the present passage may be either the elements of learning or the elemental spirits. If Paul was using the word in the former sense (the elements of learning), the whole statement means that the Gnostic system, though represented by its proponents as advanced "philosophy," was really only rudimentary instruction, the ABC's of the world (cf. TCNT: "puerile questions of this world"). That is to say, it was elementary rather than advanced; it was earthly rather than heavenly.

The rendering "elemental spirits" (cf. RSV, Moffatt) is, however, to be preferred. Understood in this manner, the passage means either (a) that the "philosophy" of the errorists was a system instigated by the elemental spirits (perhaps thought of as the powers of evil) or (b) that it was a system having the elemental spirits as its subject matter. Meaning (b) is more likely the one intended by Paul, for we know from 2:18 that the Colossian heresy made much of the "worship of angels."

"Of the world" marks the elemental spirits as concerned with visible and perishable things, not with the abiding realities which are ours in Christ.

Third, it was a system *not after* [*according to*] Christ (v. 8d). This is Paul's most telling criticism of the teaching at Colossae. The thought may be that the Colossian heretics put the elemental spirits in the place which in Christianity is reserved for Christ. That is, they made the elemental spirits, not Christ, central in their system. In this interpretation there is the suggestion that Christ alone is deserving of the supreme place in our thought and worship. Another, and perhaps better, interpretation takes this phrase to mean simply that the teaching of the heretics did not accord with the truth as it is revealed in Christ. Following this interpretation we may derive the principle that Christ is the pole-star of theology, the standard by which all doctrine is to be measured. Any system, whatever its claims or pretensions, is to be rejected if it does not conform to the revelation which God has given us in Him.

2. *The justification of the warning* (vv. 9-15). Paul's warning rests on the fact of Christ's unshared supremacy (v. 9) and His complete adequacy to meet human need (vv. 10-15). Because of who He is and what we find in Him any system "not after Christ"

must be wrong. The passage takes up the central phrase of 1:19 ("fulness") and draws out its consequences in relation to the Colossian heresy. Bruce gives his discussion of it the heading "Christ is all—and all you need" (p. 228).

Our discussion centers in three profound affirmations which are here made about Christ. These are:

(1) *The full deity of Christ: For in him dwelleth all the fulness of the Godhead* (v. 9, ASV). Nearly every word in this statement is significant. "For," linking this and the following verses to verse 8, shows that the warning of that verse rests upon what is said here about Christ and His fullness. The phrase, "in him," by its position within the sentence, is emphatic, the thought being that in Christ alone the fullness of deity dwells. "Dwelleth" (cf. 1:19) translates a word which suggests taking up permanent residence. The tense is present, stating a general truth and denoting continuous action. The full thought, then, is that in Christ the fullness of deity permanently resides, finding in Him "a settled and congenial home" (H. C. G. Moule, p. 144). The context, however, suggests that the primary reference is to Christ in His present glorified state.

"Fulness" translates the same word which was found earlier in 1:19. Here it is defined by the addition of the phrase "of the Godhead." These latter words translate a term found only here in the New Testament, though a similar, but weaker, word (denoting "divine nature") is found in Romans 1:17. The word employed in the present passage is an abstract term, betokening not just divine qualities and attributes but the very essence of God. H. C. G. Moule explains it to mean "the whole glorious total of what God is, the supreme Nature in its infinite entirety" (p. 144).

The gnostic teachers asserted that deity was filtered through a succession of spirit powers (angelic beings). Paul denies this by affirming that the Godhead in "all" its fullness dwells in Christ. Phillips: "It is in him that God gives a full and complete expression of himself."

(2) *The real humanity of Christ:* the fullness of the Godhead dwells in Him *bodily* (v. 9), that is, in incarnate fashion.[1] The fullness of Deity resided in the preincarnate Word (cf. John 1:1 ff), but not in bodily fashion. At Bethlehem, however, the Word was

[1] Lightfoot, Abbott, and others think this is the only tenable view of the passage. It is surely the most obvious meaning. There are, however, many who look at it differently. Calvin, for instance, prefers to interpret "bodily" to mean "substantially," "truly, really, in opposition to *typically, figuratively*" (p. 183). Scott and Beare use the terms "really," "genuinely." Peake, following Haupt, understands the sense to be "as a complete and organic whole" (p. 524).

clothed with flesh and made God "gloriously tangible and accessible to us" (H. C. G. Moule, p. 144).

In our concern for the truth of Christ's deity we are sometimes tempted to undervalue His humanity. We must insist on the reality of both truths. Christ is fully God—very God of very God—yet He is really man, one with us. This is an emphasis particularly prominent in Hebrews and is a truth which we must guard and cherish.

(3) *The complete adequacy of Christ: And in him ye are made full, who is the head of all principality and power* (v. 10, ASV). This statement crowns Paul's argument. The meaning is that because Christ is fully God and really man we, in union with Him, "are made full," that is, we share in His fullness. The words "in him," denoting vital union with Christ, are by their position in the verse emphatic. The sense is that only as we are joined to Christ is this fullness ours.

"Ye are made full," writes Calvin, "does not mean that the perfection of Christ is transfused into us, but that there are in him resources from which we may be filled, that nothing be wanting to us" (p. 183). The main idea, then, is that in union with Jesus Christ our every spiritual need is fully met. Possessing Him, we possess all. There is no need, therefore, for the Christian to turn to any other source for spiritual help. Specifically, Paul intended his readers to understand that it was foolish for them to turn to the philosophy of the Colossian heretics, the ritual of the Mosaic law, or to the spirit-beings (angelic powers) worshiped by the pagan world. All they needed was in Jesus Christ. As Wesley put it, "Thou O Christ art all I need, More than all in Thee I find."

The all-sufficiency of Christ is further affirmed in the statement that He is "the head of all principality and power" (v. 10b). He is "the head" in the sense that He is the source of life for, and sovereign Lord over, all that exists. Whatever powers there may be in the universe, whatever ranks and orders of authority and government, they all owe their being to Christ and are under His lordship.

The thought of Christ's sufficiency, expounded in detail in verses 11-15, is pointed up by the mention of three things which Christ (or God in Christ) has done for us. These have to do with (1) spiritual circumcision (vv. 11, 12), (2) forgiveness of sins (vv. 13, 14), and (3) victory over the forces of evil (v .15).

(1) In Christ we have true circumcision (vv. 11, 12). The essential statement of this is in verse 11a: *In whom ye were all*

circumcised with a circumcision not made with hands (ASV). "In whom" means in union with Christ, joined to Christ. The "circumcision not made with hands" is obviously intended to contrast the Christian's circumcision with the circumcision required by the Mosaic law (and preached also by the errorists of Colossae). That circumcision, which represented the cutting away of man's uncleanness and was the outward sign of one's participation in Israel's covenant with God, was made with hands (i.e., was physical) and affected an external organ of the body. The circumcision which the believer experiences in Christ is spiritual, not physical, and relates not to an external organ but to one's inward being. In short, it is what elsewhere in Scripture is designated circumcision of the heart (Rom. 2:28f; cf. Phil. 3:3). The tense of the verb ("were ... circumcised") is aorist, pointing to the time of conversion.

Paul further describes this circumcision as consisting *in the putting off of the body of the flesh* (v. 11b, ASV). The Greek word for "putting off," a double compound, conveys the ideas of putting (stripping) off and of casting away. The imagery is that of discarding—or being divested of—a piece of filthy clothing.

"The body of the flesh" has been variously explained, but of the many explanations proposed only two seem worthy of consideration. One is that which takes "body" to denote something like "mass" or sum total, "flesh" to denote evil nature. Calvin, a proponent of this view, interprets the entire phrase as expressing the "accumulation of corruptions" (p. 184). Scott, in similar fashion, defines it as meaning "the whole carnal nature" (p. 44); Beare uses the expression, "the whole of our lower nature" (p. 197). The renderings of Weymouth and Norlie reflect this interpretation.

The other view understands "body" to be a reference to the physical body, "flesh" to be a descriptive genitive marking the body as *conditioned by* our fallen nature. The "putting away" of the body, according to this interpretation, speaks of "finding in Christ strong deliverance from the assaults of evil" which come through the body, of experiencing "a wonderful emancipation from the clinging power of temptation through the body" (H. C. G. Moule, pp. 150, 151). This is the thought reflected in TEV: "freed from the power of this sinful body." See also TCNT, which speaks of throwing off "the tyranny of the earthly body."

Having described the believer's circumcision as inward and spiritual and as consisting of the putting off not of a part of the flesh but the whole body of the flesh, the apostle now brings forward a third characteristic: it is *the circumcision of Christ* (v. 11c). This obviously is not a reference to the circumcision experienced *by* Christ in His infancy; nor is it, as some contend, an expression for the death of Christ. It is a reference to and a description of something experienced by the Christian. Assuming this to be true, we may interpret the genitive ("of Christ") in either of two ways. It may, for instance, be taken as a simple possessive. The meaning then is that the circumcision under discussion belongs to Christ (i.e., is Christian circumcision), and thus is to be distinguished from the circumcision of, that is, belonging to, Moses. It is better, however, to take the genitive as subjective and to understand the whole phrase as speaking of a (spiritual) circumcision *performed* by Christ on the believer at the time of conversion. The two interpretations, in the final analysis, are not radically different.

Verse 12, a further explanation of the spiritual circumcision affirmed in the preceding verse, suggests that the believer's baptism is the "outward counterpart" to that experience and as such is the means by which it is openly declared. Perhaps the thought of "burial" in baptism was suggested by the previous mention of the "putting off" of "the body of the flesh." The emphasis of the verse, however, is not on the analogy between circumcision and baptism; that concept is soon dismissed, and the thought shifts to that of baptism as symbolizing the believer's participation in the burial and resurrection of Christ.

In the reference to being *buried with him in baptism,* etc., the imagery is not simply that of burying an old way of life and rising to a new kind of life; it is rather that of sharing in the experience of Christ's own death and resurrection.

That Paul did not think of baptism as actually effecting participation in that experience is made clear when he adds that Christians are raised *through faith in the working of God.* (v. 12b, ASV). Baptism, then, is not a magic rite, but an act of obedience in which we confess our faith and symbolize the essence of our spiritual experience. Faith is the instrumental cause of that experience, and apart from real faith, baptism is an empty, meaningless ceremony.

"Faith in the working of God" is the rendering of a Greek construction which, translated literally, reads "through the faith of the working of God." The phrase may be interpreted in either of two ways. For instance, it could mean "the faith which is *the effect of* the working of God." Luther, Bengel, and many other older commentators understood it in this fashion. This is also the view reflected in Conybeare's rendering: "wherein also you were made partakers of His resurrection, through the faith wrought in you by God" (cf. Weymouth, who translates similarly). Others construe the phrase to mean faith which is *directed toward,* or exercised in, the mighty power by which God raised Christ from the dead (cf. Eph. 1:19, 20). There is much to be said for both of these interpretations, but perhaps it is better to follow the second. This is the view advocated by most modern interpreters and is the understanding expressed in ASV, RSV, NEB, TCNT, Goodspeed, and other versions.

"Working" (KJV: "operation") renders the Greek word from which we get the word "energy." Goodspeed translates it "power"; TCNT, "omnipotence." The NEB is perhaps best: "active power."

(2) In Christ we have forgiveness (vv. 13, 14). The fact is stated in verse 13: *And you, being dead through your trespasses and the uncircumcision of your flesh, you, I say, did he make alive together with him, having forgiven us all our trespasses* (ASV). The closing words of verse 12 have mentioned God's raising Christ from the dead. Now the apostle assures his readers that in Christ they share the resurrection experience. In Christ's case it was a literal bodily resurrection from the dead. In their case, the death was spiritual ("dead through your trespasses," etc.), and the being made alive is also spiritual. (Eventually, of course, believers will experience a bodily resurrection. The resurrection of Christ, who is "the first fruits" of those who sleep in death, is the pledge of their resurrection. And in Paul's thought the future glorified life is the continuation of the spiritual life imparted to believers in conversion.)

"Dead in your sins and . . . uncircumcision" (KJV) suggests "sins" and "uncircumcision" as the sphere in which death was manifested. This is the interpretation expressed also by Conybeare: "dead in the transgressions and uncircumcision of your flesh." It is better, however, to follow the ASV and understand the Greek to mean dead *through* or *by reason of* trespasses and uncircumcision.

The word for "trespasses," which literally means "a falling beside," suggests failure to follow the path charted for man by God. It speaks therefore of a deviation from uprightness and truth.

If we follow KJV ("dead *in* . . . uncircumcision") "the uncircumcision of your flesh" may be interpreted literally, the reference being to the Colossians' Gentile extraction (cf. Eph. 2:11).

If we follow ASV (*"through* . . . uncircumcision") the phrase cannot be taken literally, for physical uncircumcision did not actually separate the Colossians from God and did not really contribute to their spiritual deadness. We are required then to interpret the phrase in a spiritual sense, understanding it to mean something like "unregenerate nature." The TCNT renders it "uncircumcised nature." Outward circumcision, which marked the Colossians' real separation from Israel, was also a *symbol* of their alienation from God. The figurative use of the term "circumcision" in this passage is therefore quite legitimate and readily understood. (Compare Acts 7:51, where it is said of Jews that they were "uncircumcised in heart and ears.")

If "uncircumcision" is taken in the sense of "paganism," the phrase could then be understood as denoting either the sphere ("in") or the instrumental cause ("through") of death, for this term has for us something of the same double connotation which "uncircumcision" conveyed to Jewish minds.

"Did . . . make alive,"[2] translating an aorist tense, refers to the time of the Colossians' conversion. In saying that they were made alive "together with" Christ Paul emphasizes their participation with Christ in His resurrection (cf. Eph. 2:5). The words do not mean, however, that Christ and the Colossians were quickened in the same manner. They rather express the idea of fellowship. The new life that was theirs not only was made possible by Christ; it was shared with Him.

The first part of verse 13 affirms the readers' deadness through trespasses and their being made alive in union with Christ. *Having forgiven us all our trespasses* (v. 13b, ASV) indicates that their being made alive involved the forgiveness of everything which had once alienated them from God.

Perhaps "forgiving" is a better translation than "having forgiven," for the experience of forgiveness is simultaneous with the quickening. Forgiveness and quickening are in fact "the same act of divine grace viewed under a different but complementary aspect" (Beare, p. 198). The Greek word, built on the root of the word for "grace," means literally "to grant as a favor." The term was sometimes used for the cancellation of a debt (Luke 7:42, 43). Perhaps its use here, however, simply points to divine grace as the root principle in forgiveness.

It is of interest that in the best texts (cf. ASV, RSV, etc.) the pronoun following "having forgiven" is the first person ("us").

2 Biblical scholars debate whether God or Christ is to be thought of as the subject of the verb "made alive." Chrysostom, Ellicott, and others argue for Christ as subject; most interpreters today prefer to think that God is subject of the verb. Likewise it is felt that God is the One acting in the expressions "having forgiven" and "having blotted out."

In this manner Paul expresses his participation with the Colossians in the blessing of forgiveness.

Verse 14 vividly describes the attendant circumstances of forgiveness in Christ: *"having blotted out the bond written in ordinances that was against us, which was contrary to us: and he hath taken it out of the way, nailing it to the cross* (v. 14, ASV). "Having blotted out" suggests that this act is the grounds for forgiveness. Perhaps it would be better to translate it "blotting out," and understand it as specifying the act by which the forgiveness was carried out. At any rate, the word expresses one feature of the forgiveness of trespasses which believers experience. The strict meaning of the Greek term is "to wipe out" or "wipe away" (cf. Acts 3:19: Rev. 3:5; 7:17; 21:4). In secular literature it was used of blotting out a writing or of abolishing a law. Cancellation is the idea here.

What is cancelled is called "the bond written in ordinances." The word translated "bond" (lit., "handwriting," KJV) was used of any document written by hand. Exactly how Paul uses the term is not certain. Scott, for example, points to its use in ancient times for an indictment drawn up against a prisoner and understands the apostle to be employing the word similarly. Barclay calls it "a self-confessed indictment," "a charge-list which, as it were, they themselves had signed and had admitted was accurate" (p. 170). This is the idea reflected in Phillips' rendering: "Christ has utterly wiped out the damning evidence of broken laws and commandments." Others point to the use of the word for a note of hand, an I.O.U. Bruce calls it a "signed confession of indebtedness" (p. 238). Goodspeed's version reflects this interpretation: "He . . . canceled the bond which stood against us." Either way, the reference is to the Mosaic law; and whether it is thought of as a bond of indebtedness or as an official indictment, the thought is that God has blotted it out so that it no longer stands against us.

Three expressions are used to describe the law: (1) It was "written in ordinances." That is to say, it was expressed in decrees or commandments (cf. Eph. 2:15). The TCNT renders it "the bond that consisted of ordinances"; RSV, "the bond . . . with its legal demands." Barclay understands it to mean "based on the ordinances of the law" (p. 168). (2) It was "against us." That is to say, God's law had a valid claim on us. It was (if we follow the imagery of a "bond") like a promissory note having our signature attached as evidence that we acknowledged its claim and our debt. (3) It was "contrary (directly opposed) to us." This suggests that because we could not meet the claims of the law, it was hostile toward us.

Verse 14a has asserted that this bond has been "blotted out"; verse 14b now adds that it has been "taken . . . out of the way," and "nailed" to the cross. "Hath taken" (Phillips: "has completely annulled"), the rendering of a perfect indicative, emphasizes abiding results. The bond (the Mosaic law) has been removed permanently, that is, removed so that its claims against us can never again alienate us from God. "Nailing," an aorist participle, indicates the means by which it has been removed. In addition, the figure may serve to emphasize still more the permanence of the removal.

The metaphor of nailing the law to the cross has been variously explained. Some, for instance, think there is an allusion to an ancient custom which dictated that when decrees were nullified, a copy of the text should be nailed up in a public place. On the other hand, Scott, who interprets the "handwriting" as an indictment, sees here an allusion to the custom of hanging over the head of an executed person a copy of the charge on which he was condemned. When Jesus was crucified, the superscription nailed to His cross contained the words, "The King of the Jews." Paul "boldly ignores the real superscription, and imagines the Law as nailed above the cross. This, on the deeper view," explains Scott, "was the charge on which Christ was put to death. He suffered in order to satisfy in our stead 'the indictment which was against us' and has thus set it aside" (p. 47). Barclay, whose interpretation is somewhat like Scott's, understands the idea to be that the indictment was itself crucified.

To sum up, the great principle asserted in verse 14 is the destruction of the law in and by the cross of Christ. The law, however, appears to be viewed in a certain character (i.e., as a bond of indebtedness or as an instrument of condemnation, something that stood "against us," was hostile toward us). It stands here, as H. C. G. Moule says, for "the covenant broken by the sinner, and therefore turned into his mortal foe, his sentence of second death" (p. 156).

Maclaren mentions three ways in which the cross is the end of law: first, it is the end of the law's power of punishment. Second, it is the end of the law as ceremonial. Third, it is the end of the law as moral rule. This, he explains, does not mean that the Christian is free from the obligations of morality. It does mean that he is not bound to do the things contained in the law just because they are there.

> Duty is duty now because we see the pattern of conduct and character in Christ. Conscience is not our standard, nor is the Old

Testament ideal of manhood.... Our law is the perfect life and death of Christ who is at once the ideal of humanity and the reality of Deity.

The weakness of all law is that it merely commands but has no power to get its commandments obeyed. Like a discrowned king it posts its proclamations, but has no army at its back to execute them. But Christ puts His own power within us, and His love in our hearts; and so we pass from under the dominion of an external commandment into the liberty of an inward spirit. He is to His followers both "law and impulse".... He came "not to destroy, but to fulfill." The fulfillment was destruction in order to reconstruction in higher form. Law died with Christ on the cross in order that it might rise and reign with him in our inmost hearts (pp. 217-220).

(3) In Christ we have victory, for He has conquered all the powers of evil: *having despoiled the principalities and the powers, he made a show of them openly, triumphing over them in it* (v. 15, ASV). The meaning of nearly every word of this verse is disputed. One of the key issues concerns the interpretation of "principalities and powers." Space does not permit discussion of the various views. The one preferred here is that which sees "the principalities and powers" as hostile angelic powers, what H. C. G. Moule calls "the dreadful hierarchy of evil" (p. 158). The words include all the spiritual forces of this world which are in rebellion against God, designated elsewhere as "the world-rulers of this darkness" (Eph. 6:12, ASV; cf. Col. 1:16; 2:8, 19, RSV). There is doubtless an allusion to the supernatural powers which figured so prominently in the gnostic system.

Paul affirms that Christ has "despoiled" these forces of evil. The Greek verb, which is in the middle voice, is interpreted by some to mean "having stripped off from' himself," as though the principalities and powers had attached themselves to the Son of God in determination to bring about His destruction. Christ strips them from Himself like a wrestler casting from himself a disabled antagonist. This interpretation, strongly urged by Lightfoot, is reflected in several of the versions (cf. Weymouth, TCNT, NEB). Perhaps it is better to construe the middle as intensive; the meaning then is simply "having stripped," and the object of the action is not "himself" but the principalities and powers. In this interpretation the imagery is that of a conquered antagonist being stripped of his weapons and armor and put to public shame. Conybeare renders it, "He disarmed the Principalities and the Powers."

Paul goes on to say that Christ, having thus stripped the principalities and powers, "made a show of them openly." That is to say, He exposed them to public disgrace, made them a public spectacle by exhibiting them to the universe as His captives.

The added words, "triumphing (exulting) over them in it," expand this idea. The picture, one quite familiar in the Roman world, is that of a triumphant general leading a parade of victory. The conquering warrior, riding at the front in his chariot, leads his troops through the streets of his home city. Behind them trails a wretched company of vanquished kings, officers, and soldiers — the spoils of battle. Christ, in this picture, is the conquering general; the principalities and powers are the vanquished enemy displayed as the spoils of battle before the entire universe.

The final word, "it," though capable of being rendered as masculine ("him") is best understood as a reference to the cross. To the casual observer it seemed to be only an instrument of death, the symbol of Christ's defeat. But Paul represents it as Christ's chariot of victory. The meaning is that it was by His death that Christ conquered His enemies, stripped them of their power, exposed them to public disgrace, and led them in His own triumphal procession.

II. THE WARNING AGAINST LEGALISM (2:16, 17).

The preceding paragraph has dealt with "the philosophy" of the Colossian heretics. Now (2:16-23) the apostle brings in their religious practices. There is no elaborate discussion of these; only brief notices are given, with warnings that the erroneous practices are to be avoided.

Verses 16, 17 are a warning against legalism: *Let no man therefore judge you in meat, or in drink, or in respect of a feast day or a new moon or a sabbath day: which are a shadow of things to come; but the body is Christ's* (vv. 16, 17, ASV). "Therefore" shows that this and the following warnings grow out of the statement of Christ's complete sufficiency made in the preceding verses. There is perhaps special reference to His removal of the law and His triumph over the forces of evil (vv. 14, 15). In light of that the Colossians were to let no one "judge" them in reference to their observance or non-observance of the regulations of the Mosaic law. The thought seems to be that no one is to be permitted to use these things as a basis for judging the believer's standing before God. For "judge," TCNT has "take you to task"; Weymouth, "sit in judgement on."

"Meat" (lit., "eating") and "drink" (lit., "drinking") are probably references to the dietary rules set out in the Mosaic law about clean and unclean food. It is possible, however, that Paul was not thinking of Jewish law at all, but simply of the peculiar ascetic tendencies of the Colossian heresy. If this line of interpretation is followed, the question is not one of lawful and unlawful foods but of eating and drinking as opposed to abstinence. Peake, who is an advocate of this view, writes: "Asceticism rather than ritual cleanness is in his [Paul's] mind" (p. 5:30).

"Feast day," "new moon," and "sabbath" refer of course to various holy days of the Jewish calendar — annual, monthly, and weekly. Paul's thought seems to be that the Christian is freed from obligations of this kind (cf. v. 14). No one, therefore, should be permitted to make such things a test of piety or fellowship (cf. Rom. 14:1ff.). "The new religion," Eadie explains, "is too free and exuberant to be trained down to 'times and seasons.' ... Its feast is daily, for every day is holy; its moon never wanes, and its serene tranquillity is an unbroken Sabbath" (p. 177).

All such legal stipulations, Paul declares, are but "a shadow [i.e., an anticipation] of the things to come." "The body," that is, the reality or "substance" (Moffatt), belongs to Christ. The thought is that in Him we have the reality of which these other things were but a prefigurement. In Christ, the things to come have come.

These two verses, writes H. C. G. Moule, are

> an appeal for "Christian liberty," as earnest, though less in passion, as [Paul's] appeal to the Galatians "not to be entangled again in the yoke of bondage." But let us note well that the "liberty" he means is the very opposite of licence and has nothing in the world akin to the miserable individualism whose highest ambition is to do just what it likes. The whole aim of St. Paul is for the fullest, deepest and most watchful holiness. He wants his Colossian converts above all things to be holy; that is, to live a life yielded all through to their Redeemer, who is also their Master (p. 171).

III. The Warning Against Worship of Angels (2:18, 19).

Paul's third warning brings before us two of the most puzzling verses in the New Testament: *Let no man rob you of your prize by a voluntary humility and worshipping of the angels, dwelling in the things which he hath seen, vainly puffed up by his fleshly mind, and not holding fast the Head, from whom all the body, being supplied and knit together through the joints and bands, increaseth with the increase of God* (vv. 18, 19, ASV). The Greek expression for "let no man rob you of your prize" has been rendered in many different ways: KJV, "beguile you of your reward"; Williams, "defraud you as an umpire"; Knox, "cheat you"; C. F. D. Moule, "declare you disqualified" (p. 104). The literal meaning is "let no one act as umpire against you," that is, give an adverse decision against you. Bruce concludes that the expression is simply a strong way of saying "let no one judge you" (cf. v. 16). Beare, in similar fashion, says the term expresses more picturesquely the same thought as the verb in verse 16. The essential meaning is, let no one deny your claim to be genuine Christians.

The means by which the false teachers were attempting to do this was by imposing "a voluntary humility and worshipping of the angels" on the Colossian Christians. "Voluntary humility" is a particularly difficult expression. "Humility," in this context, must be a mock humility. NEB: "self-mortification"; RSV: "self-abasement." "Voluntary" (used in KJV and ASV) apparently means something like "self-imposed." The Greek word, a participle whose literal meaning is "willing," may be rendered "delighting in" (cf. RSV, "insisting on"). Others, construing it closely with the verb, think it has adverbial force, meaning something like "willingly," "arbitrarily." This idea is reflected in Moffatt's rendering: "Let no one lay down rules for you *as he pleases*" (italics mine).

"Worshipping of the angels" is an allusion to the deference paid by the gnostic teachers to the hierarchy of spirit beings which, in their system, filled the whole universe. Perhaps the "humility" and the "worshipping of the angels" were closely related. That is to say, the Gnostics probably insisted that their worship of angels rather than the supreme God was an expression of humility on their part. H. C. G. Moule quotes Quesnel, a Roman Catholic, as saying that "Angels will always win the day over Jesus Christ despised and crucified, if the choice of the mediator . . . is left to the vanity of the human mind" (p. 177).

"Dwelling in the things which he hath seen"[3] gives another attendant circumstance of the attempt to rob the Colossians of their prize. The meaning, according to some, is that the heretical teacher takes his stand on his (imaginary or alleged) visions (cf. RSV). In Dargan's words, he "harps" upon his visions, "telling more than he or anybody else can prove" (p. 38). Barclay uses the expression, "making a parade of the things which he has seen"

[3] The KJV translates a text which employs a negative and thus changes the meaning entirely: "intruding into those things which he hath *not* seen." The thought expressed by this reading is that the false teacher deals with mysteries of which he has no immediate knowledge. Lightfoot suspects that the Greek text may be corrupted here and proposes that the reading might originally have been a construction which he translates "treading the void" (p. 197).

(p. 175). Others think there is an allusion to the initiatory rites of the mystery cults and that Paul is scornfully quoting some of the jargon ("entering in," "what he has seen") used by the heretical teachers (cf. Beare, p. 204).

"Vainly puffed up by his fleshly mind" gives Paul's appraisal of the heretical teacher. "Puffed up," which renders a term suggesting a pair of bellows, depicts him as inflated with conceit. "Vainly" indicates that his conceit is groundless (RSV: "without reason"). The "fleshly mind" is a mind dominated by the unrenewed nature; it is therefore a mind which "lacks spiritual enlightenment" (Beare, p. 204).

Still another description of the false teacher is found in verse 19: "not holding fast the Head." Here the assertion is that the false teacher lacks vital contact with Jesus Christ. This is profoundly serious because it is from Christ as Head that "all the body [the church], being supplied and knit together through the joints and bands, increaseth with the increase of [wrought by] God." Each believer is thought of as forming a vital connection with Christ the Head. Thus joined to Him, they all become the joints and ligaments by which the whole body (the church) is supplied with energy and life. The heretical teacher, without this contact with Christ, cannot possibly contribute to the growth of the church.

IV. THE WARNING AGAINST ASCETICISM (2:20-23).

Paul's fourth and final warning is against ascetic restrictions (man-made rules imposed as a means of gaining favor with God). The ascetic sees the body as evil and concludes that the way to holiness is to deny all of the body's desires, refuse its appetites, and cut its needs down to an irreducible minimum. The body is, for the ascetic, a thing to be punished and buffeted, a thing to be treated as an enemy. Asceticism was apparently a prominent feature of the Colossian heresy, and it has had strong appeal for misguided people in many periods of history. The third and fourth centuries, for instance, were times when asceticism was extremely widespread. People starved themselves until they became emaciated. To bathe or otherwise care for the body was thought of as sinful; consequently, it was not uncommon for one so to neglect his body that it became a breeding place for lice. One writer speaks of lice dropping from people as they walked, a condition looked upon as a sign of special holiness.

It was the ascetic spirit which led to the deprecation of marriage, the exaltation of virginity and monasticism, and the devising of endless means of self-torture. Maclaren, commenting on the appeal of asceticism, remarks that "any asceticism is a great deal more to men's taste than abandoning self. They will rather stick hooks in their backs and do the 'swinging poojah,' than give up their sins or yield up their wills" (p. 2). Paul condemns asceticism and urges the Colossians to reject it as a way of life. He mentions, in support of his view, (1) the Christian's death to the rudiments of the world (vv. 20-22a), (2) the human character of ascetic rules (v. 22b), and (3) the ineffectiveness of asceticism to check the indulgence of the lower nature (v. 23).

1. *The Christian's death to the world* (vv. 20-22a). When one becomes a Christian, his connection with the world of legal and ascetic ordinances is severed. Asceticism, then, is not in keeping with the nature and circumstances of the new life in Christ. All of its rules and requirements are a kind of anachronism for the Christian. *"If ye died with Christ from the rudiments of the world, why, as though living in the world (i.e., why, as though you had never died), do ye subject yourselves to ordinances?"* (v. 20, ASV). The "if" clause, a first-class condition in Greek, is not intended to express doubt or uncertainty. Its force is argumentative, and the meaning is: "since (because) you died" (cf. TCNT). The use of this type of conditional clause is Paul's emphatic way of stating something which is unquestionable (cf. 3:1; Phil. 2:1, etc.). The tense of the verb is aorist, pointing to the time of the believer's conversion.

However, in the mention of dying (v. 20) and rising (3:1) with Christ, there is perhaps an allusion to the believer's baptism, an experience in which his body is buried beneath the water and then is raised, as it were, out of a watery grave (cf. Rom. 6:3ff.). Baptism, though, only *pictures* the believer's death to an old way of life and his rising to a new life. The actual change is wrought when he is joined to Christ by faith. In that experience he enters into fellowship with Christ, and in dying with Him is delivered from the rudiments of the world. "Rudiments" has here the same ambiguity which marks it elsewhere (cf. discussion at v. 8). Perhaps it should be understood as a reference to the supernatural powers of evil (cf. RSV), but the passage also yields an acceptable meaning if "rudiments" is interpreted in the sense of elementary instruction. At any rate, to order life by ascetic rules is to revert to an inferior state one supposedly abandoned at the time of conversion. To die from the rudiments of the world is to have all connections with them severed, to be done with them, to be liberated from their authority.

"Subject yourselves to ordinances," which translates a single Greek word *(dogmatizesthe)*, recalls verse 14, where reference was made to the blotting out of the bond of ordinances *(dogmata)* against us. To "subject yourselves to ordinances" is to permit life to become again a round of rules. The "ordinances" which Paul had in mind in the present passage are such decrees and commandments as *handle not, nor taste, nor touch* (v. 21, ASV). The reference is to the dietary restrictions which the errorists imposed as a means of attaining salvation. Some may have been reenactments of the Mosaic law; others were doubtless prohibitions stemming from pagan asceticism. There is a descending order in the terms, the climax being reached in the last word: "Don't even touch."

Parenthetically Paul adds that all such things *are to perish with the using* (v. 22a, ASV). That is to say, the things with which such commandments as "handle not, nor taste, nor touch" have to do are actually made to be used; and with the use they perish, for food ceases to be food once it is eaten (cf. TCNT). The underlying thought then is that the restrictive regulations of the Colossian heresy deal with matters that are fleeting and unimportant. Christ, in fact, has made all foods clean (Mark 7:19).

2. *Ascetic restrictions of human origin* (v. 22b). Such regulative prohibitions as "handle not, nor taste, nor touch" are *after the precepts and doctrines of men.* Knox: "based on the will and the word of men." The essential thought is that the rules of the ascetic are, both in origin and in medium of communication, strictly human.

3. *Ascetic restrictions ineffective* (v. 23). Paul affirms that the rigid restrictions of asceticism *have indeed a show of wisdom in will-worship, and humility, and severity to the body; but are not of any value against the indulgence of the flesh* (v. 23, ASV). The expression, "have a show of wisdom," means that the ascetic rules masquerade as wisdom. They seem, on the surface, to be reasonable and wise. But what seems to be wisdom is only an appearance of, or pretention to, wisdom. In reality they are expressions of "will-worship" and spurious "humility."

"Will-worship" denotes a self-imposed worship, "a devoteeism invented and elaborated by human choice" (H. C. G. Moule, p. 181). Calvin defines it as a "voluntary service, which men choose for themselves at their own option, without authority from God" (p. 202). Eadie, in similar fashion, speaks of it as worship "unsolicited and unaccepted" (p. 205). The context suggests that the errorists engaged in such "worship" in the hope that they would thereby acquire superior merit before God. The Greek word is a rare compound used in the New Testament only here; it calls to mind the reference to "worship of angels" in verse 18.

"Humility," in this context, must refer to a mock humility (cf. v. 18). The TCNT: "so-called 'humility'." The idea is that asceticism, while parading under the guise of humility, actually panders to human pride.

"Severity (lit., "unsparingness") to the body" is a reference to ascetic torturings of the body.

"Are not of any value against the indulgence of the flesh"[4] translates a very difficult Greek construction which has given rise to many different interpretations. The two that have the most to commend them are those expressed in the rendering of ASV and in the rendering of Moffatt. In either interpretation "flesh" stands for the old sinful nature.

To sum up, verse 23 teaches that such restrictions as "handle not," "taste not," "touch not" have the appearance of wisdom for many people in that they seem to be expressions of devotion to God, of humility, and of a commendable discipline of the body. Paul, however, declares that these regulations have nothing to do with real wisdom, and the worship and humility which they profess to express are both spurious. His final appraisal is that asceticism is a dismal failure. On the surface it may appear to be the way to spiritual victory, but it really is not. One can punish his body to the limit and can still have a heart filled with unconquered lusts.

Before leaving this section, we may, in light of its teachings, make several observations.

1. We must not think of Christianity as a rule-book religion. That is, we must not interpret it to be a religion of prescriptions but a religion of a living relationship with Jesus Christ. Even the ethical portions of the New Testament do not consist of mere rules and regulations; at bottom the instructions given there are the expression of deep and abiding spiritual principles. Moreover, since Christianity is a religion of relationship to Christ, it is a religion of freedom — freedom from external laws and man-made rules (cf. Gal. 5:1ff.). This, of course, does not mean that once we are in Christ everything is permissible. That would amount to

---

[4] The ASV is the version we have quoted in the discussion. In Moffatt's version the clause reads: "but they are of no value, they only pamper the flesh!" (cf. RSV margin). This interpretation is the one preferred by many able commentators.

moral and spiritual anarchy, a thing contrary to the very nature of the new life in Christ. It does mean that the controls of the Christian life spring from within. Indwelt by the Spirit, we walk by the Spirit and thus avoid carrying out the desires of the lower nature (Gal. 5:16).

2. We must not confuse legitimate Christian discipline with the man-made rules of asceticism. It is one thing to live an ordered Spirit-controlled life (cf. Gal. 5:16ff), born of a desire to be more like God; it is another thing to impose the austerities of asceticism upon one's self as a means of gaining salvation.

3. We must remember that the prohibitions of asceticism lack the power either to maintain the Christian life or to promote its growth. Genuine piety grows out of inward conviction generated by a consciousness of union with Christ.

For Further Study

1. After reading and studying Colossians 2:8-23, write out in your own words some of the leading errors of the false teaching at Colossae.

2. Use a concordance to study the word "rudiments" in Paul's epistles. Check various translations, particularly NEB and RSV for other renderings.

3. Study the idea of triumph or victories in Paul's writings.

CHAPTER 6

The Life of the Christian

(Colossians 3:1—4:6)

In the preceding portion of Colossians, the apostle has refuted both the doctrinal and practical errors of the false teachers and, in the course of doing this, has given a profound exposition of the cosmic significance of Jesus Christ. In the present section, which is practical and ethical in its emphasis, he exhorts his readers to give outward expression in daily life to the deep experience which is theirs in Christ. The Christian life is a life "hid with Christ in God," but it is still, Paul explains, a life lived out on earth. The Christian must therefore give attention not only to his inward experience with God but also to his outward relations with his fellowman. No explicit references to false teachers are made, but we may assume that what is here said about the pursuit of a life of holiness is set against the opposite tendencies of the Colossian errorists.

The air of controversy hangs heavy over all of the first half of the epistle, and its style, reflecting this, is abrupt and broken. In the last half of the book, marked by simplicity of style and language, there is a more tranquil tone.

The structure of the passage now to be considered is quite simple. Beginning with a brief but all-encompassing statement of the root principle of the Christian life (3:1-4), the apostle proceeds to delineate some practical guidelines for living that life (3:5—4:6). Our discussion is built around these two themes.

I. THE ROOT PRINCIPLE OF THE CHRISTIAN LIFE (3:1-4).

The opening verses of chapter 3 sustain the closest connection with the closing verses of chapter 2. There the apostle reminds the Colossian Christians that ascetic regulations are of no real value against the indulgence of the flesh. The only remedy for sinful passions is found in the believer's experience of union with

Christ — a union by virtue of which the Christian dies to sin and to the world's way of thinking and doing. The opening verses of the third chapter, representing the positive counterpart of those verses, teach that this death with Christ involves also participation in His resurrection life. This releases into the believer's life a power that is more than adequate as a check against fleshly appetites.

These four verses, then, point to the believer's union with Christ as the root principle of the whole Christian life. It is the point of departure and the source of power for all that we do.

On the basis of this mystical but real experience with Christ the Colossians are urged to seek heavenly things (v. 1) and to set their minds on heavenly things (v. 2). As a further incentive to carrying out these injunctions, they are reminded that their lives are now securely hidden with Christ in God and thus belong to the invisible realm. Their sphere of being, action, and enjoyment is therefore now totally different from that of their former state (v. 3). Believers' lives, however, will not always be hidden. There is concealment now, but when Christ appears there shall be glorious manifestation (v. 4).

H. C. G. Moule calls this "one of the golden paragraphs of the whole Bible. To countless hearts," he observes, "it is one of their peculiar treasures. There is a celestial music for them in its very phrase and rhythm" (p. 189). Our discussion focuses upon the two appeals of the passage (to seek the things above, v. 1, and to set the mind on things above, v. 2) and the three motivations for carrying out these actions (vv. 1, 3, 4).

1. *Seeking the things above* (v. 1). To *seek the things that are above* (ASV) is to desire, to strive for the things above. It is to see to it that our interests are centered in Christ, that our attitudes, our ambitions, and our whole outlook on life are molded by our relation to Him. Calvin explains that "we seek those things which are above when in heart and spirit we are truly sojourners in this world and are not bound to it."

The "things that are above" (used in verse 2 in contrast with "things upon the earth") designates heavenly (spiritual) things, the things *where Christ is* (v. 1, ASV). Perhaps Paul gives concrete expression to these things in the catalogue of virtues set forth in 3:12-17.

The description of Christ as *seated on the right hand of God* is another tacit rejoinder to those who were seeking to diminish Christ's role as mediator, for the right hand of God is a figurative expression for the place of supreme privilege and authority. There is the additional thought in the phrase that Christ, thus exalted, is in position to intercede for us and to supply our every need.

2. *Setting the mind on things above* (v. 2). Seeking the things above is descriptive of the aim, the practical pursuit of the Christian life. Setting the mind on things above refers more to inner disposition. There is, of course, an intimate connection between the two. Eadie comments that "the sure safeguard against seeking things below, is not to set the mind upon them" (p. 215).

To set the mind on things above means, among other things, that we are to give such things a large place in our thinking. This, of course, does not mean that we are to withdraw ourselves from all of the activities of this world and do nothing but contemplate eternity and heaven. The injunctions given by Paul in the verses that follow make it quite clear that he expected Christians to maintain the normal relationships of this world. "But," as Barclay explains, "there will be this difference — from now on the Christian will see everything in the light and against the background of eternity. He will no longer live as if this world was all that mattered; he will see this world against the background of the larger world of eternity" (p. 177).

Setting the mind on things above means more, however, than just thinking about heavenly things. Included is the obligation to make sure that the bent of our inner nature, the tendency of our thought and will is toward God.

The things that are upon the earth (v. 2) might include material wealth, worldly honor, power, pleasures, and so forth. To make such things the goal of life and the substance of contemplation is unworthy of one who has been raised with Christ and anticipates sharing in His eternal glory. "The pilgrim," writes Eadie, "is not to despise the comforts which he may meet with by the way, but he is not to tarry among them, or leave them with regret" (p. 215).

3. *The motivations for these actions* (vv. 1, 3, 4). Three motivations are given for seeking and setting the mind on the things above. One is our union with Christ in resurrection: *if then ye were raised together with Christ,* etc. (v. 1a, ASV). This clause should be compared with the opening words of 2:20. There the apostle spoke about death with Christ; here he speaks of our life with Christ. The "if" here, as there, is not intended to express doubt. It introduces a type of conditional clause which assumes the reality of the condition and might be translated "since." The NEB expresses its force by the rendering, "Were you not raised to life with Christ?"

A second motivation for seeking and setting the mind on heavenly things is expressed in verse 3: *for ye died, and your life is hid with Christ in God* (ASV). This verse in a sense repeats and summarizes the idea expressed in 2:20. In the present context the thought is that since Christians have died with Christ all that is alien to Him should be foreign to them.

Death with Christ (2:20) was followed by resurrection with Christ (3:1), and so our lives "are hid with Christ in God." H. C. G. Moule adds: "There it lies, and there it lives; and so if you would *live it out,* using this wonderful life-power for spiritual triumph and service here on earth, you must go evermore to find it there; you must 'seek' it; you must 'with him continually dwell', in steadfast recollection, simplest reliance, and ceaseless secret reception of the divine supply" (p. 188).

The idea of life being hidden with Christ suggests not only the security of the believer's life, but also that it belongs in a very real and profound sense to the invisible realm. Eadie, observing that the words "hid with Christ," etc., are placed in contrast with open manifestation at Christ's second advent, thinks the idea of concealment is the main point of the statement. Our present connection with God and Christ, he explains, is "a matter of inner experience — not as yet of full and open manifestation" (p. 217).

The third motivation to seeking and setting our minds on the things above is the prospect of our future manifestation with Christ in glory. *"When Christ, who is our life, shall be manifested, then shall ye also with him be manifested in glory* (v. 4, ASV). As H. C. G. Moule writes, "You shall be manifested with Him, He shall be manifested in you. See that you use Him as your life today, in the uplifting hope of such a to-morrow" (p. 189).

Christ is called "our life" because He is, quite literally, the essence of our life. It is He who gives us life and fans and fosters it by His abiding presence within us. "If Christ be in you, the body is dead because of sin; but the Spirit is life because of righteousness" (Rom. 8:10).

"Shall be manifested," a reference to the return of Christ, is a translation of one of several Greek terms used in the New Testament for this event. *Parousia* (often rendered "coming") speaks literally of Christ's (future) presence with His people. *Epiphaneia* ("manifestation," "appearance") points up the visibility and splendor of His coming *Apokalupsis* ("revelation") denotes the inner meaning of the event. *Phaneroo,* the word employed here, emphasizes its open display.

II. Guidelines for the Christian life (3:5—4:6).

In the preceding paragraph (3:1-4), which is preparatory to what is said here, Paul has reminded his readers of their vital union with Christ and the power and encouragement which this gives to holy living. Indeed, the believer's union with Christ is represented in those verses as the fundamental and controlling principle of the new life. The present passage (3:5—4:6), which shows in a practical way how that principle is to be applied, offers straightforward guidance for realizing the divine ideal of Christian holiness. In short, the apostle teaches that the Christian's experience in Christ calls not simply for regulating the old earthbound life but for digging out its roots and utterly destroying it. In this way the new life in Christ will have free course and will attain full dominion. The underlying thought is: Let the life that is in you by virtue of your union with Christ work itself out and express itself in every thought, deed, and relationship.

The passage before us combines moral instruction and authoritative commands. Many separate ideas are presented, but the main message of the passage may be summarized under its four leading appeals. These have to do with the abandonment of the vices of the old life (3:5-11), the cultivation of the virtues of the new life (3:12-17), the strengthening of family relationships (3:18—4:1), and the performance of religious duties (4:2-6).

1. *The vices of the old life to be abandoned* (3:5-11). The Colossians had only recently come out of a paganism which condoned the grossest of sins. It was therefore most appropriate that Paul should speak forthrightly about the demands of the new life and the urgent need to repress all the degrading tendencies of the old nature. The three imperatives of the paragraph ("put to death," v. 5; "put . . . away," v. 8; and "lie not," v. 9) are the pegs on which the thought hangs.

(1) *Vices to be put to death* (vv. 5-7). *Put to death* [i.e., *treat as dead*] *therefore your members which are upon the earth* (v. 5a, ASV). In principle the Colossians had, in becoming Christians, died with Christ (cf. 2:20; 3:3). Now they are charged to make this death to the old life real in everyday practice. The verb, meaning literally "to make dead," is very strong. It suggests that we are not simply to suppress or control evil acts and attitudes. We are to wipe them out. "Slay utterly" may express its force. The form of the verb (aorist imperative) represents the action as something to be undertaken decisively, with a sense of urgency.

The expression "members which are upon the earth" is defined by the list of sins (3:5b) placed in apposition with it. Paul is calling, then, not for the maiming of the physical body but for the slaying of the evil passions, desires, and practices which root themselves in, make use of, and attack us through, our bodies. H. C. G. Moule calls it "a bold but intelligible transition of thought" which gives "a more concrete effect to the mental picture" *(Cambridge Bible,* p. 121). It is as though the apostle had written, "When I speak of putting your members to death, I mean put to death fornication, uncleanness, etc., of which the members of your bodies are instruments." Weymouth, attempting to soften the figure, interprets the term to mean "your earthward inclinations." Goodspeed has "your physical nature." The TCNT understands it to mean "all that is earthly in you"; NEB, "the parts of you that belong to the earth."

The catalogue of sins explaining "members upon the earth" is a grim one: *fornication, uncleanness, passion, evil desire, and covetousness* (v. 5b, ASV). All of these, with the possible exception of the last, have to do with sexual vice. "Fornication" translates the most general Greek word for illicit sexual intercourse. Originally it denoted the practice of consorting with prostitutes; it came eventually to mean "habitual immorality." Several of the versions (Williams, Phillips, etc.) render it "sexual immorality." It was a sin woefully rife in Paul's day, and for that reason was by him ruthlessly condemned.

"Uncleanness," though sometimes used of physical impurity (Matt. 23:27), here has a moral connotation. Including uncleanness in thought, word, and act, it has a wider reference than the word for "fornication." The NEB renders it "indecency"; Phillips calls it "dirty-mindedness."

The word for "passion" which essentially means "feeling" or "experience," was used by the classical writers of any passive emotion, whether good or bad. However, it came to be specially used of violent emotions. In the New Testament, where it always has a bad sense, it means uncontrolled desire. The term following ("evil desire") is similar but perhaps more general in meaning. The noun ("desire") denotes strong desire of any kind. The adjective ("evil") shows that the thing here condemned is desire for the wrong things.

The Greek word for "covetousness," a compound form whose root meaning suggests a desire *to have more,* has a much wider significance than its English equivalent. Souter's *Lexicon,* calling it "a word active in meaning, and wide in scope," defines it as "greediness, rapacity, entire disregard of the rights of others." Some interpreters think the context gives support to the view that greed for sex is the meaning here. But perhaps it is better to retain the more usual meaning and understand it as a ruthless desire for and seeking after material things. E. K. Simpson says the related word in Ephesians 5:5 means "money-grubber" *(N.I.C., N.T.)* and suggests that the word has overtones of exploitation. Phillips renders the term used in this passage as "lust for other people's goods." This attitude is identified with *idolatry* because the lust for wealth puts things in the place of God.

Verses 6 and 7 mention two factors which point up the impropriety of such sins in the lives of believers. First, they are the things for which *cometh the wrath of God upon the sons of disobedience* (v. 6, ASV). The "wrath of God" is understood by some as a reference to a general principle in life. Barclay, for instance, says the wrath of God is simply "the rule of the universe that a man will reap what he sows, and that no one ever escapes the consequences of his sin. The wrath of God and the moral order of the universe are one and the same thing" (p. 183). Similarly, C. F. D. Moule interprets the term here to denote a principle of retribution and suggests that it might be rendered as "disaster from God" (p. 117). There is truth in this view, but perhaps it is better to interpret Paul's term of the eschatological wrath of God. "Cometh," a present tense, may represent God's judgment upon sin as already on the way, but more likely the present tense is used in a futuristic way to depict more vividly the certainty with which God's judgment will fall upon the disobedient.

A second matter which points up the impropriety of the presence of these sins in Christians' lives is that they are the vices which characterized and belonged to their pre-Christian experience: *wherein ye also once walked, when ye lived in these things* (v. 7, ASV). The two verbs, both past tenses, emphasize that this kind of life belongs to the past and that the Christian should be done with it. "Walked," an aorist tense in Greek, has summary force. That is to say, it gathers up their whole life as pagans and focuses it in a point. "Lived," an imperfect tense, stresses the course and habit of their existence. "In these things" refers to the vices listed above and represents them as the moral atmosphere of the Colossians' pre-Christian lives.

(2) *Vices to be put away* (v. 8). Whereas the sins of verse 5 had to do with impurity and covetousness, the catalogue of verse 8 concerns sins of attitude and speech. *But now do ye also put them*

*all away: anger, wrath, malice, railing, shameful speaking out of
your mouth* (v. 8, ASV). "But now" marks an emphatic contrast
with the reference in the preceding verse to the former life of the
Colossians. The imagery in "put . . . away" is that of putting off
clothes. The suggestion is that Christians are to divest themselves
of sins just as one might strip off of himself a filthy garment.

It is debated whether the injunction to put away refers to the
vices mentioned in verse 5 or to the vices following (v. 8b). Perhaps the term has both a forward and a backward reference, but
it seems mainly to point forward. The things to be put away then
are "anger, wrath," and so forth.

The first three terms — "anger," "wrath," "malice" — speak of
sins of disposition. Scholars are not in agreement on the distinction, if any, between the words for "anger" *(orgé)* and "wrath"
(thumos). The view which is perhaps most widely held looks upon
"anger" *(orgé)* as the settled feeling of anger, and "wrath" *(thumos;*
Moffatt, "rage") as the sudden and passionate outburst of that
feeling. Others, however, take the opposite view. They see the
latter word *(thumos,* "wrath") as the inner emotion and the former
(orgé, "anger") as the outward expression. One argument in support of this is the fact that the word for "anger" *(orgé)* in verse 8
is the same as the word for "wrath" *(orgé)* in verse 6, and unquestionably verse 6 uses the term for the external manifestation
of wrath. C. F. D. Moule, who thinks it is difficult to press any
distinction in the meanings of the words in the present verse,
points out that in the Septuagint the terms are virtually
synonymous.

"Malice" is a general term for wickedness or badness. Here it
seems to denote a vicious disposition or spite, the spirit which
prompts one to injure his neighbor (cf. Goodspeed, Knox). The
TEV renders it "hateful feelings"; Weymouth, "ill-will."

"Railing" and "shameful speaking" both have to do with speech.
"Railing" (KJV, "blasphemy") renders a word which denotes insulting and slanderous talk. When used of insulting speech directed
against God, it means blasphemy. In the present passage, where
it seems to be used of insulting talk directed against men, it should
be understood in the sense of "slander."

"Shameful speaking" may denote either filthy or abusive speech,
and the authorities are divided as to its meaning here. Moffatt,
Knox, RSV, and NEB interpret in the former sense; TCNT and Goodspeed express the latter meaning. Perhaps the former (i.e., "filthy

speech") is the meaning intended here. Weymouth, following Lightfoot, combines both ideas: "foul-mouthed abuse."

"Out of your mouth" probably qualifies both "railing" and "shameful speaking." The expression vividly depicts these as pouring out of the mouth.

(3) *A vice to be discontinued: Lie not one to another* (v. 9a). Scott thinks the sin of falsehood is singled out for special mention because in it more than in anything else we manifest ill-will toward our fellow men. At any rate, the fact that the sin of lying is given separate treatment makes the condemnation of it more emphatic. The verb, unlike those in verses 5 and 8, is present imperative, which with the negative forbids the continuance of the act. Williams therefore renders it, "Stop lying."

Verses 9b, 10 express reasons for being done with the vices listed above. (The strict grammatical connection of these verses is with the prohibition against lying, but probably there is a sense-connection with the total thought of vv. 5-9a.) The essence of it is that the Christian has had a radical, life-changing experience in which he *put off the old man with his doings* (i.e., habits or characteristic actions) and *put on the new man* (ASV). The metaphor again is one of clothing. The "old man" (i.e., the old, unregenerate self; RSV, "old nature") is like a dirty, worn-out garment which is stripped from the body and thrown away. The "new man" (i.e., the new, regenerate self; RSV, "new nature") is like a new suit of clothing which one puts on and wears. The picturesque language gives vivid expression to a great truth, but one must be careful not to press the imagery too far.

The new man (self) is described as *being renewed unto knowledge* (ASV). The essential thought is that the new self (nature) does not decay or grow old but by constant renewal takes on more and more of the image of its Creator. The tense of the participle ("being renewed") is present, expressing a continuous process of renewal. "Knowledge," which is represented as the goal of this process, denotes true knowledge (cf. 1:9). H. C. G. Moule understands it to include "the regenerate man's spiritual vision of Christ, intimacy with Him, insight into His will" *(Cambridge Bible,* p. 125).[1]

Verse 11, rounding out this paragraph, declares that in the realm of the new man — that is, where the image of God is truly

---

[1] For the idea of renewal see Romans 12:2; 1 Corinthians 4:16. For the thought of creation in the "image" of God see Genesis 1:26-28.

reflected in men — distinctions of race, class, and culture are artificial and have no real significance. Such differences, to be sure, remain in the Christian community, but not in such a way as to be barriers to fellowship. To the extent that Christians do permit them to be barriers, they are acting out of character.

The various groups mentioned have to do with ·distinctions of national privilege *(Greek and Jew)*, legal or ceremonial standing *(circumcision and uncircumcision)*, culture *(barbarian and Scythian,* the latter thought of as the lowest of the barbarians), and social caste *(bondman, freeman)*. The obliteration of such distinctions was one of the most remarkable achievements of the Gospel.

In affirming that *Christ is all, and in all* Paul means that Christ is the great principle of unity. In Him all differences merge, all distinctions are done away. C. F. D. Moule, who thinks this phrase ought not be too precisely analyzed, looks on it as "a vigorous and emphatic way of saying that Christ is 'absolutely everything' " (p. 121). Phillips' rendering expresses the same thought: "Christ is all that matters, for Christ lives in them all." The paraphrase of *The Living Bible* is similar: "Whether a person has Christ is what matters, and he is equally available to all."

2. *The virtues of the new life to be cultivated* (3:12-17). The Christian has already put on the new man (the regenerate nature, v. 10). Now he must clothe himself (cf. TCNT) with the garments which befit the new man. *Put on* (v. 12) should be compared with the terms "put to death" (v. 5) and "put away" (v. 8). Those terms express the negative, this verse the positive aspects of the Christian's reformation of character. The tense of the verb, an aorist imperative, speaks of an action to be undertaken with a sense of urgency.

As an incentive to the carrying out of his appeal Paul reminds his readers that they are *God's elect, holy and beloved* (v. 12, ASV). These descriptive terms, all used in the Old Testament of Israel, emphasize the favored position now enjoyed by the Colossian Christians. They are the heirs of Israel's spiritual privileges. As God's "elect" they are His chosen ones. "Holy," which comes from the same root word which is rendered "saints" in 1:2, marks the Colossians as set apart for, consecrated to, God. "Beloved" is a reminder that they are dear to God. Paul's appeal is based, then, on this threefold fact: Christians are chosen of God, set apart by and for God, and loved by God. The three terms signify essentially the same great fact, but under different aspects.

The virtues with which Christians should clothe themselves are listed in verses 12b-17. Those in verses 12b-14, which have to do mainly with relationships among Christians, fall under the regimen of "put on" (vv. 12, 14). This group reaches its climax in the mention of love, and all of them are in some way expressions of love. Verses 15-17 depict the elevated frame of mind which should characterize those who profess to be Christ's people. The ideas expressed in these verses are given more individual treatment, each for the most part being associated with its own imperative verb.

(1) *Expressions of love* (vv. 12-14). Verse 12b contains a pentad of great Christian virtues which must be "put on": *a heart of compassion, kindness, lowliness, meekness, longsuffering* (ASV). They point up those qualities of life which, if present in the community of believers, will eliminate or at least reduce frictions. All of them are manifestations of love, which is mentioned as the crowning virtue. Some interpreters (e.g., Scott and Beare) think this grouping is the counterpart to the five vices which, in verse 8, we are told to "put off."

"A heart of compassion" (lit., "bowels[2] of mercies," KJV) betokens pity and tenderness expressed toward the suffering and miserable. C. F. D. Moule calls it "ready sympathy" (p. 123).

The word for "kindness" combines the ideas of goodness, kindliness, graciousness. Ellicott defines it as "sweetness of disposition" (p. 181). In Romans 11:22 it is contrasted with "severity." In Galatians 5:22 it is listed as a fruit of the Spirit.

"Lowliness" and "meekness," which are related terms, were not considered virtues in the pagan world. The New Testament, however, deepened and enriched their meanings and made them two of the noblest of Christian graces. The former word, which originally meant servility, came to denote a humble disposition — "the thinking lowly of ourselves because we are so" (Ellicott, p. 182). "Meekness," the opposite of arrogance and self-assertiveness, is the special mark of the man who has a delicate consideration for the rights and feelings of others. Combining the ideas of gentleness and submissiveness, it is mentioned in the New Testament as a characteristic of Christ (Matt. 11:29), a fruit of the Spirit (Gal. 5:23), a distinctive trait of those who belong to Christ (Matt. 5:5), and so on.

"Longsuffering," a word of frequent occurrence in the New Testament epistles, denotes the self-restraint which enables one to

---

2 "Bowels," though the literal meaning of the Greek word, is better expressed by "heart." The ancients thought of the lower viscera as the seat of emotions. We, however, use "heart" in this sense.

bear injury and insult without resorting to hasty retaliation. The Bible mentions it as an attribute of God (Rom. 2:4) and as a fruit of the Spirit (Gal. 5:22).

Verse 13a uses two participles *(forbearing* and *forgiving)* to expand upon the thought of "longsuffering." That is to say, the man who is truly longsuffering will manifest this attitude in at least two ways: (a) by his willingness to bear with those whose faults and unpleasantness are an irritant to him and (b) by his willingness to forgive those against whom he has grounds for complaint.

"Forbearing" suggests the thought of putting up with things we dislike in others. Moulton speaks of the failure of Christians to practice this as "probably the most prolific cause of Christian division" (p. 52). "Forgiving," which translates a word used in 2:13 of God's action toward us, has the sense of forgiving *freely.*

One another and *each other* suggest that the need for forbearance and forgiveness within the Christian fellowship is mutual.

Verse 13b states one of the great incentives to forgiveness: *even as the Lord forgave you, so also do ye.* Knox's version is expressive: "the Lord's generosity to you must be the model of yours."

The final article of Christian attire is love: *And above all these things put on love, which is the bond of perfectness* (v. 14, ASV). All of the virtues listed in verses 12, 13 are, on the highest level, manifestations of love; but love is larger than any one of them, indeed, larger than all of them combined. The mention of love as a separate "article of clothing" is therefore not superfluous. The Greek word is *agape,* the distinctive Christian term for caring love.

"Above all" may mean "in addition to all" or, carrying on the metaphor of clothing, "over all," "on top of all." Perhaps the latter is the better way of interpreting the phrase.

The genitive ("of perfectness") is taken by some to be an appositive. The meaning then is "the bond which is (or consists in) perfection."[3] Others construe the genitive to be objective. "Perfectness" in this interpretation is that which is bound.[4] Still others interpret

---

[3] Peake, who interprets in this fashion, understands love to be perfection in the sense that it binds the members of the Christian community together. "When love binds all Christians together," he explains, "the ideal of Christian perfection is attained" (p. 541).

[4] Lightfoot, who is an advocate of this view, takes "perfectness" to be a designation of all the virtues. Love as the bond of perfectness, then, is "the power which unites and holds together all those graces and virtues which together make up perfection" (p. 222).

the genitive to be descriptive. The meaning then is "the bond *characterized* by perfectness," that is, the perfect bond. This is the view which, on the whole, seems best. "Love" is the perfect bond (belt) in the sense that it embraces and completes all of the other virtues. Conybeare's rendering expresses this meaning: "which binds together and completes the whole."

(2) *The rule of peace* (v. 15). *And let the peace of Christ rule in your hearts, to the which also ye were called in one body* (ASV). Those who see this verse as a continuation of the appeal for loving concern (v. 14) among Christians are inclined to interpret "peace" to mean peace between the members of the Christian community. Scott, for example, defines it as "a peace-loving temper, inspired by Christ" (p. 75). Chrysostom illustrates it as follows: "Suppose a man to have been unjustly insulted, two thoughts are born of the insult, the one urging him to vengeance, and the other to patience, and these wrestle with one another. If the peace of God stand as umpire, it bestows the prize on that which calls for endurance, and puts the other to shame" (quoted by Eadie, p. 247).

Those who understand the verse as introducing a new idea interpret "peace" as inward "heart" peace. Eadie defines it as "that calm of mind which is not ruffled by adversity, overclouded by sin or a remorseful conscience, or disturbed by the fear and the approval of death" (p. 247). C. F. D. Moule explains it as "the peace which is the result of obedience" to Christ (p. 124). Perhaps we should not limit the word but should understand it as including peace in the largest sense. Peace (i.e., a peace-loving temper) is to be the principle which governs our actions and our words, but that it might do this the "peace that passeth all understanding" must first govern in our hearts.

It is the peace "of Christ" because it is the peace given by Him (cf. John 14:27). For the peace of Christ to "rule" in our hearts is for it not simply to be present but to exercise supreme control within us. The word for "rule," an expressive term used only here in the New Testament, originally meant "to act as umpire." The scholars are not in agreement as to whether the word in Paul's time retained the connotation of a contest or was used simply in the general sense of administering, ruling, or deciding. (A compound form of this word is used in 2:18). The essential meaning here is that in all inner conflicts as well as in all disputes and differences among Christians, Christ's peace must give the final decision. Nothing is to be done which would violate that peace. Goodspeed's rendering expresses it well: "Let the ruling principle in your hearts be Christ's peace." The TCNT: "Let the Peace that the Christ gives decide all doubts within your hearts"; Weymouth, "settle all questionings within your hearts."

As an incentive for living by this principle Paul reminds his readers that it was to peace that they *were called in one body* (v. 15b). That is, they were so called that they constitute one body, and peace should be the life-spirit which animates them.

Be ye thankful is added not as an afterthought but because gratitude is so intimately associated with peace. The sense may be that we are to be grateful for the calling that is ours (mentioned in the phrase which immediately precedes), the suggestion being that God has ordered all things for our welfare. More likely, the meaning is that we are to be grateful for the peace which Christ bestows on us (which is the main idea of the verse). Thankfulness for this peace becomes an incentive for preserving it. It is possible that the injunction should be taken in its broadest sense: Be thankful — both to God and to men. Such gratitude surely promotes peace and harmony within a fellowship.

The word for "thankful" was sometimes used in the sense of "pleasant" (cf. Prov. 11:16, Septuagint). This meaning, while not entirely inappropriate in the present passage, is rejected by most interpreters. The verb ("be") may be rendered "become," the suggestion being that it is a habit (present tense) which must be acquired. Knox: "Learn, too, to be grateful."

(3) *The indwelling of Christ's word* (v. 16). All of the preceding appeals (with the possible exception of that in v. 15) have to do largely with duties we owe to one another. Verses 16 and 17 focus attention on matters which have to do more directly with our own personal life. Even here, however, the thought of our duty to others is not entirely absent.

The word of Christ probably refers to the Gospel, that is, the message about Christ. It may, however, refer to Christ's teaching. Lightfoot, who sees no direct reference in the phrase to any definite body of truths (written or oral), interprets it as "the presence of Christ in the heart, as an inward monitor" (p. 224).

To let the word of Christ *dwell in you richly* is to let it "have ample room" (Berkeley) or to let it "remain as a rich treasure" (Weymouth; cf. NEB) in the heart. The general sense is that we are to submit to the demands of the Christian message and to let it be so deeply implanted within us that it controls all our thinking. "Let it dwell not with a scanty foothold, but with a large and liberal occupancy" (Eadie, p. 250).

The correct punctuation of the remainder of verse 16 is uncertain. The ASV, Weymouth, RSV, NEB, and others construe *in all wisdom* with the words following. The KJV and Phillips take the phrase with the words preceding. Much can be said for either construction. Our preference is for the former. The meaning, however, is not radically affected.

One other matter relating to punctuation: It appears that a break (perhaps a semicolon) should be made after the words *one another* (cf. RSV). The thought of the verse then is that under the influence of the word of Christ Christians are to do two things: (a) In all wisdom (i.e., making use of every kind of wisdom) they are to teach and admonish one another. (b) Using psalms, hymns, and spiritual songs, they are to sing with grace in their hearts to God.

Rigid distinctions should not be made between *psalms, hymns,* and *spiritual songs*. The language is intended to emphasize rich variety of song, not to give instruction in ancient hymnody. Essentially the three terms are employed to heighten the idea of joyousness called for in the passage. If any differentiation is made, "psalms" may be taken to refer to the Old Testament psalter; "hymns" and "spiritual songs" both refer to distinctly Christian compositions, the latter possibly being impromptu rhythmic utterances produced under the influence of the Holy Spirit.

Grace translates a term which may mean either grace or gratitude (depending upon the context in which it occurs). If the former sense is given the word, the meaning may be something like "under the inspiration of divine grace," or "by the help of divine grace." In spite of the fact that this is the more frequent sense of the Greek word, many able interpreters prefer to take it here to mean gratitude (cf. RSV, NEB, NAB, Moffatt, et al.).

(4) *The name of Christ* (v. 17). The last verse of the paragraph under consideration is brought in as a sort of summary statement: *And whatsoever ye do, in word or in deed, do all in the name of the Lord Jesus, giving thanks to God the Father through him* (ASV). Doing all "in the name of" the Lord Jesus is interpreted in at least three ways. Some, for instance, understand the meaning to be that everything the Christian does is to be undertaken in an atmosphere of prayer, so that he may be assured of Christ's presence and help. Moffatt expresses this meaning: ". . . let everything be done in dependence on the Lord Jesus." Others think the meaning is that everything the Christian does is to be done in recognition of the authority of Christ's name. Eadie, a proponent of this view,

states it thus: "To speak in His name, or to act in His name, is to speak and act not to His honour, but under His sanction and with the conviction of His approval" (p. 254). Still others take "in the name of the Lord Jesus" to mean "as followers of the Lord Jesus" (cf. Goodspeed; *The Living Bible).* This interpretation reflects the thought that to act in the name of a person is to act as his representative (cf. prayer "in the name of" Jesus). The sense then is that in all the relationships of life we are to act with an awareness that we are Christ's people. Both of the last two interpretations are acceptable, but the third is to be preferred.

"Giving thanks" indicates an attendant circumstance of acting in the name of the Lord Jesus. That is to say, in all that we do we are to have an abiding sense of God's goodness to us and are to be careful to thank Him.

3. *Family relationships to be strengthened* (3:18—4:1). Several observations may be made as we approach this important paragraph. First, it may be seen as applying in a specific way the general principle laid down in verse 17. Indeed, it shows how all of the graces enjoined in verses 12-17 express themselves within the family circle. Paul would probably have agreed with the statement that "Christian thinking has not become really Christian until it operates in our daily practice with those nearest to us" (Moulton, p. 56).

Second, the emphasis of the whole passage is on *duties,* not rights. The rights, to be sure, are clearly implied in all that is said, but the stress does not fall on these. To be specific, when Paul addresses wives he does not remind them of their rights (though he unquestionably recognized that they had rights); he talks rather of the wife's duty to her husband. The same approach is taken in addressing husbands, parents, children, slaves, and masters. A home is on shaky ground when the members of the family are constantly thinking of and insisting on their rights. If each person will be solicitous of his duty toward others, the rights will be cared for.

Third, the duties are shown to be reciprocal. That is, all of the rights are not on one side and all the duties on the other. No, if the wife has her duty, the husband has a corresponding duty. If the children have their duties toward parents, the parents have reciprocal duties toward the children. The same principle applies to slaves and masters.

Fourth, the entire passage is remarkably similar to, though much briefer than, that found in Ephesians 5:22ff. Both passages deal with the same relationships: wives, husbands; parents, children;

slaves, masters. The chief difference is that in Ephesians Paul introduces a rather lengthy statement about the church as the bride of Christ.

(1) *The wife's duty to the husband* (3:18). The one duty which Paul puts upon the wife is submission: *Wives, submit yourselves unto your own husbands, as it is fit in the Lord* (KJV). The main thought is that the wife is to defer to, that is, be willing to take second place to, her husband. H. C. G. Moule thinks the meaning is something like "be loyal to." Phillips translates it "adapt yourselves to." In essence the words are a specific application of the principle stated in Romans 12:10: "in honor preferring one another."

This injunction must not be interpreted in such a way as to suggest that the husband is a domestic despot, ruling his family with a rod of iron. It does suggest, however, that the husband has an authority which the wife must forego. In areas where one must yield — for example, the husband's choice of a profession or of a geographical location for his work — the primary submission must devolve upon the wife.

Three things may be said about the wife's subjection to her husband. First, the context indicates that the wife's attitude is prompted by and warranted by the husband's unselfish love.

Second, the form of the verb (middle voice) shows that the submission is to be voluntary. That is to say, the wife's submission is not something forced upon her by a demanding husband; it is the deference that a loving wife, conscious that home (just as any other institution) must have a head, gladly shows to a worthy and devoted husband.

Third, such submission is said to be "fitting in the Lord" (ASV). The verb has in it the thought of what is becoming and proper. The phrase "in the Lord," to be construed with "is fitting," indicates that wifely submission is proper not only in the natural order (as pagans would teach) but also in the Christian order. The whole thing, then, is lifted to a new and higher level. The TCNT translates it "as befits those who belong to the Lord."

(2) *The husband's duties to the wife: Husbands, love your wives, and be not bitter against them* (v. 19, ASV). The ancient world was a man's world, and in no place was this more apparent than in the home. Even among the Jews the wife was often little more than chattel. And in the Greek home the women of the household were confined to their own quarters, not even permitted to eat their meals with the men. Paul's counsel in the present passage is in

striking contrast to all of this, for he recognizes that the husband, no less than the wife, has duties within the home.

The text sets out two such duties, one positive and the other negative. Positively, Paul enjoins husbands to "love your wives." This of course is their supreme duty. The word employed does not denote mere affection or romantic attachment; it is the term which denotes caring love, a deliberate attitude of mind which concerns itself with the well-being of the one loved. Self-devotion, not self-satisfaction, is its dominant trait. It is, in short, a love which makes it a delight for the wife to subject herself to such a husband.

Negatively, husbands are exhorted to "be not bitter against" their wives. The term suggests a surly, irritable attitude. Perhaps the colloquial expression "don't be cross with" expresses the meaning better than the expression "be not bitter." The TCNT renders it "and never treat them harshly."

(3) *The duty of children to parents: Children, obey your parents in all things, for this is well-pleasing in the Lord* (v. 20, ASV). The one duty here enjoined upon children is that of obedience to their parents. It is a timely word for a day which tends to regard the freedom of the child as an absolute. The word translated "obey" implies a readiness to hear and has in it the sense of obeying orders. The thought is that the child is to listen to and carry out the instructions of his parents. The tense of the verb is present, indicating that such action is to be habitual.

Two things are said about the obedience which children owe to their parents. First, it is to be complete: "in all things." Eadie comments: "The principle involved in [Paul's] admonition is, that children are not the judges of what they should or should not obey in parental precepts" (p. 260). Paul, of course, sets this whole passage in a Christian context. That is to say, he is dealing with the *Christian* home and does not contemplate unchristian attitudes on the part of parents. As Abbott points out, "There would be no propriety in suggesting the possibility in a Christian family of a conflict between duty to parents and duty to God" (p. 293).

Second, the obedience of children to their parents is "well-pleasing in the Lord" (ASV). (Compare the similar statement in v. 18b.) Perhaps the meaning is that in the Christian order, just as in the order under the law or in the natural realm, obedience to parents is pleasing to God.[5] Filial obedience, therefore, is not

---

[5] The TCNT gives a slightly different turn to the phrase: "for that is pleasant to see in those who belong to the Lord."

based on anything accidental, nor does it depend essentially on the character of the parent. It is an obligation grounded in the very nature of the relationship between parents and children. It is, as the parallel passage in Ephesians clearly states, a thing in itself right. It is therefore especially pleasing to God when believing children are careful to fulfill this duty. Moffatt: "for this pleases the Lord right well."

(4) *The duty of parents to children: Fathers, provoke not your children, that they be not discouraged* (v. 21, ASV). The specific mention of "fathers" suggests that the father as head of the household has a special responsibility in regard to the training of the children. No slight toward the mother is intended. Paul would surely have been quick to recognize her rights and the molding power of her influence in the home. It is possible that the word "fathers" is used here in the broad sense of "parents." (Compare Heb. 11:23, where the same Greek word is used of the two parents of Moses.)

The teaching of this verse should be compared with the parallel statement in Ephesians 6:4: There the thought is cast in a more positive form, the emphasis being upon the responsibility of parents to develop character in their children. In the present passage the underlying idea is that parents are to see to it that they deserve the obedience of their children. There may also be in it the thought that parents should strive to make obedience easy.

The essence of the counsel here is that parents should not "provoke" their children. The sense is that they are not to challenge the resistance of their children. Practically, the apostle is teaching that parents should be careful not to give in to fault-finding, nor to be always nagging their children. Weymouth renders it "do not fret and harrass your children." Phillips has "don't over-correct." Knox puts it "and you, parents, must not rouse your children to resentment."

The reason for this counsel is stated in the words "that they be not discouraged." The meaning is that parents are to deal wisely with their children, not being so exacting, so demanding, or so severe that they create within the child the feeling that it is impossible to please. The Greek word has in it the idea of "losing heart." The sense of the whole verse is well expressed by Eadie: "If children, let them do what they can, never please their father, if they are teazed *(sic)* and irritated by perpetual censure, if they are kept apart by uniform sternness, if other children around them are continually held up as immeasurably their superiors, if their best efforts can only moderate the parental frown, but never are greeted with the parental smile, then their spirit is broken, and they are discouraged" (Eàdie, p. 261). It is a situation unspeakably sad, but alas! not at all unknown among Christians. "The twig," continues Eadie, "is to be bent with caution, not broken in the efforts of a rude and hasty zeal" (p. 262).

(5) *The duty of slaves to masters* (vv. 22-25). The "servants" mentioned in these verses were bondslaves, not servants in the modern sense of the word. The duty of such slaves is dealt with in the context of the family because slaves were considered to be a part of the household.

Slavery, with all its attendant evils, was universally accepted in ancient times. In fact, it was considered a fundamental institution, indispensable to civilized society. More than half the people seen on the streets of the great cities of the Roman world were slaves. And this was the status not only of menials and craftsmen but of the majority of "professional" people such as teachers and doctors. Slaves were people without rights, mere property existing only for the comfort, convenience, and pleasure of their owners. Without question, the early Christian churches numbered many slaves among their members.

It is a matter of concern to some people that the apostles did not denounce slavery in unequivocal language and demand its immediate overthrow. The apostles, however, did not conceive of themselves as social reformers; they were first and foremost heralds of the good news of salvation in Christ. We should carefully note, though, that they did not condone slavery. Indeed, they announced the very principles (such as that of the complete spiritual equality of slave and the master) which ultimately destroyed the institution of slavery. It has been said that the approach of early Christians to this social evil was like that of a woodsman who strips off the bark of a tree and leaves it to die. John Eadie's words are apropos:

> Christianity did not rudely assault the forms of social life, or seek to force even a justifiable revolution by external appliances. Such an enterprise would have quenched the infant religion in blood. The gospel achieved a nobler feat. It did not stand by in disdain, and refuse to speak to the slave till he gained his freedom, and the shackles fell from his arms. . . . No; but it went down into his degradation, took him by the hand, uttered words of kindness in his ear, and gave him a liberty which fetters could not abridge and tyranny could not suppress (*Ephesians,* p. 446).

The phrase *masters according to the flesh* (v. 22) is Paul's way of pointing out that the slave master relationship belongs only to the sphere of earthly things. The words imply another relationship belonging to a higher, spiritual sphere where Christ is Master (cf. 4:1).

The one duty which Paul presses upon the slaves is that of obedience (v. 22) and this is to be complete ("in all things," (v. 22). Again it should be pointed out that the apostle was thinking of the *Christian* household and did not contemplate orders given to the. slave which would be contrary to the principles of the Gospel. Such orders, of course, were not to be obeyed, for our highest duty is to God, and all lesser duties must give way to this.

In verses 22b, 23 Paul urges slaves to render to their masters a service that is sincere and ungrudging. But above all they are instructed to see their lowly service as a service not rendered to men but to the Lord (v. 23b). This would transform the most menial responsibilities and give dignity to all of their work.

In verse 24 Paul reminds the slaves of the reward which shall be theirs for the rendering of faithful service in the name of Christ. Verse 25, on the other hand, shows that wrong that is done will be punished for *there is no respect of persons*. The statement is perhaps put in as a warning to the Christian slave not to presume on his position before God, thinking that God will overlook his misdeeds.

The Greek term translated "respect of persons" is variously rendered. The TCNT interprets it in the sense of partiality. Weymouth has "with God there are no merely earthly distinctions." The origin of the term is somewhat obscure but it has a connotation of showing favor to persons on account of external considerations. Three of the four New Testament occurrences of the word are in passages which assert that there is no respect of persons with God (here; Rom. 2:11; Eph. 6:9); the fourth, in James 2:1, prohibits respect of persons in God's people.

This entire statement concerning the duty of slaves may appear to be completely irrelevant to our day. There is, however, an abiding principle which may be extracted from Paul's discussion. Briefly stated, it is this: If Paul could urge slaves, who had nothing to say about the conditions and circumstances of their work, to render faithful, ungrudging service to their masters, surely he would say no less to those who today enter voluntarily into employment and who receive financial remuneration for their work. The Christian workman, like the slave of Paul's day, is to see his job as a service rendered to the Lord. This consideration will motivate him to give honest, faithful, ungrudging work in return for the pay for which his services were enlisted. Moreover, it will give him a sense of dignity in his work, regardless of how lowly it may be.

(6) *The duty of masters to slaves: Masters, render unto your servants that which is just and equal; knowing that ye also have a Master in heaven* (v. 1, ASV). This verse sets forth the duty of the master toward his slave in terms of dealing justly and equitably with him. The TCNT has "do what is right and fair." In the Roman world slaves were not thought to have rights. They were looked upon as being only animated tools. Paul, however, teaches that duty is not all on the side of slaves. Masters themselves have obligations.

The verse also contains a reason for the master's rendering to his slave what is just and equitable: "knowing that ye also have a Master in heaven." Christian masters, in other words, are reminded that they are accountable to God for their treatment of their slaves. Both they and their slaves bow alike before one Master and with Him, as noted above, there is no "respect of persons." "The gold ring of the master does not attract His eye, and it is not averted from the iron fetter of the slave" (Eadie, *Ephesians,* p. 455).

4. *Religious duties to be faithfully performed* (4:2-6). The immediately preceding paragraph (3:18—4:1) consists of a series of special appeals bearing upon the several relationships of the Christian household. In the present passage Paul returns to general counsels which apply to the entire church. Most of what is said relates to the matter of private devotion (vv. 2-4), but the unit closes with an appeal for wise behavior toward those who are not Christians (vv. 5, 6). Maclaren, commenting that the passage touches "the two extremes of life," calls his treatment of it "Precepts for the Innermost and Outermost Life." We may think of it in terms of private prayer (vv. 2-4) and public witnessing (vv. 5, 6).

(1) *The duty of prayer* (vv. 2-4). Verse 2 contains the general appeal for prayerfulness: *Continue in prayer, and watch in the same with thanksgiving* (KJV). The word for "continue," used no less than ten times in the New Testament, is translated in a variety of ways in the KJV: "continue," "continue instant," "continue steadfastly," and so forth. Built on a root meaning "to be strong," it always has a connotation of earnest adherence to a person or thing. In the present passage it implies persistence and fervor.

Weymouth: "Be earnest and unwearied." (For other uses of the word in similar settings, see Acts 1:14; 2:46; 6:5; Rom. 12:12.) Paul's injunction is in keeping with our Lord's teaching that people "ought always to pray and not lose heart" (Luke 18:1, RSV).

"Watching," which literally means "keeping awake," suggests constant spiritual alertness. The thought is that Christians must be wakeful and active in prayer, alive in the fullest sense, never careless or mechanical, never dull and heavy. The TCNT: "give your whole mind to it." Christ also emphasized the need for watchfulness in prayer (Matt. 26:41; Mark 14:38).

"With thanksgiving" refers to the pervading element in which prayers are to be offered. The cultivation of this spirit will do much to keep one alert and alive in his prayer life. Compare Moffatt's version: "Maintain your zest for prayer *by* thanksgiving" (italics mine).

Verses 3 and 4 contain the specific request that the Colossians pray for Paul, who was at this time imprisoned in Rome. The apostle's request, though mainly a personal one, was not, however, limited to himself. (Note the first person pronouns, singular and plural.) Essentially his concern was that he and his associates might have opportunity for witnessing ("a door for the word"; v. 3; cf. 1 Cor. 16:9) and that he might disclose (make clear) the great secret ("mystery") of redemption in Christ in a worthy manner (or perhaps, "as it is my duty to do," Weymouth; v. 4). The request for prayer therefore was not selfishly motivated. Paul's consuming interest was for the advancement of the Gospel, not for personal blessings.

(2) *The duty of witnessing* (vv. 5, 6). These verses, a call for discreet behavior toward the unbelieving world, may reflect the fact that charges of misconduct on the part of Christians were being circulated. It was therefore imperative that the Colossian Christians should be the more cautious, living in such an exemplary manner as to give the lie to all slanderous accusations.

Two appeals are issued, one having to do with the Christian's daily walk (v. 5) and the other relating specifically to his speech (v. 6). Solicitous attention to these matters will not only remove unbelieving suspicions about Christians but will also effectively commend the Gospel for their acceptance.

To *walk in wisdom toward them that are without* (v. 5a) is to show practical Christian wisdom in dealing with non-Christians. The words suggest that the Christian is to exhibit caution and tact so that he will not needlessly antagonize nor further alienate his pagan neighbors. In a positive sense they may also suggest that the believer is so to conduct himself that his life will attract, impress, and convict the non-Christians around him. To put it another way, Paul's concern is that the Colossian Christians live the kind of life that will give the pagan community a favorable impression of the Gospel.

Redeeming the time (v. 5b) gives an attendant circumstance of walking in wisdom. "Redeeming" comes from a market term which meant "to buy out," "purchase completely." Time is the rendering of a word which in this context means something like "opportunity." The sense of the phrase, then, is that Christians, as an expression of practical wisdom, must buy up, seize, make the most of, every opportunity for testifying to the faith. Such opportunities are brief seasons which soon pass by. The wise Christian will therefore recognize them and use them while he can.

Verse 6, with its emphasis on the Christian's speech, is perhaps brought in to point up the fact that this is an area in which he must be especially alert to opportunities for witnessing. Speech must therefore *be always with grace* and *seasoned with salt* (v. 6a).

"Grace," which in the New Testament frequently denotes divine favor, seems here to be used in a broader sense. "Pleasantness," "attractiveness," "charm," "winsomeness" — these are all ideas which may be included in the word. Eadie understands it to denote "that gracious spirit which rules the tongue, and prompts it both to select the fittest themes, and to clothe them in the most agreeable and impressive form" (p. 280).

"Seasoned with salt" may indicate that Christian conversation is to be marked by purity and wholesomeness. Some, however, understand "salt" in the sense of that which gives taste or flavor (cf. NEB, "never insipid"; Knox, "with an edge of liveliness"). Among the ancient Greeks the term was used to designate the wit which gave zest and liveliness to conversation. "Hallowed pungency" may express its meaning here.

The latter part of verse 6 tells why it is needful to cultivate speech which is gracious and seasoned with salt: *that ye may know how ye ought to answer every man* (KJV). In these words the apostle seems to say: "It all comes down to this. You need to know how to make reply to each individual. The same answer will not do in every case. Your conversation must be appropriate for, and exactly adapted to, each individual person."

FOR FURTHER STUDY

1. Read Ephesians, Colossians, and Philippians, making note of all that is said about the resurrection of Christ and our participation in it.

2. How many of the sins listed in Colossians 3:5-8 have a place in your life?

3. Study the teachings of Paul about lying.

4. Use a concordance to study the New Testament references to "new man," "old man."

5. How many of the virtues of Colossians 3:12-14 are you consciously trying to cultivate in your life?

6. Study the idea of "calling" in Paul's writings.

7. Read Colossians 3:18—4:1 and consider what you can do to make your home happier and more Christian.

CHAPTER 7

Conclusion

(Colossians 4:7-18)

The body of the letter, in which Paul has met head-on the false teachers threatening the church at Colossae, is completed. The apostle has, by a masterful exposition of the sovereign lordship and complete sufficiency of Jesus Christ, refuted their so-called "philosophy" with all its attendant errors (1:15—2:23); he has set forth the nature of the Christian life, calling attention to its springs of power, its heavenly aspirations, and its distinguishing characteristics (3:1-17); he has shown how the lofty principles of the Gospel are to affect relations within the Christian household (3:18-4:2); and he has left with his readers an earnest appeal for prayer (4:2-4) and practical advice for relating their lives properly to the pagan world (4:5, 6).

All that remains now is to give brief mention to matters of a personal nature: commendations (vv. 7-9), greetings (vv. 10-15), instructions (vv. 16, 17), and a benediction (v. 18). At least ten people, either with Paul or in Colossae, are described in one way or another in this section.

1. *Commendations* (vv. 7-9). The commendations, given to insure the proper welcome by the Colossian church, concern two men: *Tychicus* (vv. 7, 8) and *Onesimus* (v. 9). The former, who is described as Paul's *beloved brother and faithful minister and fellow-servant in the Lord* (v. 7b, ASV), was probably the bearer of both this letter and that which we know as Ephesians (cf. 6:21, 22). His name appears also in Acts 20:4 (where we learn that he was a native of Asia, the province in which Colossae was located); Titus 3:12; and 2 Timothy 4:12.

"Beloved brother" means that Tychicus is a much-loved fellow-Christian. "Faithful minister" may identify him as a loyal servant of Christ, but more likely the expression marks his relation to Paul (so Peake, Scott, et al.). Weymouth renders it "trusty assistant." The same word *(diakonos)* was earlier used of Epaphras (1:7) and of Paul (1:23). "Fellow-servant" (which, like "minister," is qualified by "faithful") speaks of Tychicus as a bondslave *(doulos)* of Christ. The prefix ("fellow") affirms Paul's sense of comradeship with him. The word was used of Epaphras in 1:7.

Paul explains that he had a twofold purpose in sending[1] Tychicus: *that ye may know our state, and that he may comfort your hearts* (v. 8b, ASV). The word for "comfort," which was used earlier in 2:2, suggests encouragement rather than consolation. The NEB: "put fresh heart into you."

Tychicus was accompanied by Onesimus, the runaway slave who in the providence of God had come into contact with Paul in Rome and (apparently through the witness of Paul) was converted to Christ. (See the epistle to Philemon for the story.) Paul now sends him back to Colossae, but no mention is made of his bondage or of his crimes of the past. Instead he is designated as a *faithful and beloved brother* (i.e., a loyal and dearly-loved fellow-believer) and as *one of you* (i.e., a trustworthy member of the community) (v. 9, ASV).

2. *Greetings* (vv. 10-15). Six persons are mentioned as sending greetings to the Colossian church. Their names may be grouped as follows:

Aristarchus, Mark, and Jesus Justus, three Jewish Christians, are listed first (vv. 10, 11). Aristarchus, a native of Thessalonica arrested at the time of the riot in Ephesus (Acts 19:29), accompanied Paul to Jerusalem (Acts 20:4) and later was with the apostle on the journey from Caesarea to Rome (Acts 27:2). He is described here as a *fellow-prisoner* (v. 10a) of Paul. The term may be interpreted either literally or spiritually (i.e., one who, along with Paul, had been taken captive by Christ). In light of the fact that Epaphras is designated in Philemon by the same term, it has been suggested by some interpreters that Paul's friends took turns in voluntarily sharing his imprisonment. There is no way of knowing that this was the case.

Mark, called here *the cousin of Barnabas* (v. 10b, ASV), is the man who wrote the gospel which bears his name. He appears in the Biblical narrative with a degree of frequency, and we know more about him than about any of the other people mentioned in the present passage.

---

[1] The Greek verb is probably an epistolary aorist, which may be rendered "I am sending" (cf. Phillips, NEB).

All that is known of Jesus Justus is what may be determined from the casual mention of his name here.

There is a note of pathos in Paul's remark that *These are the only men of the circumcision among my fellow workers for the kingdom of God* (v. 11b, RSV). The apostle felt keenly his alienation from his countrymen (cf. Rom. 9:3). But these three, he adds, *have been a comfort unto me* (v. 11c). The word for "comfort," used only here in the New Testament, is that from which the word "paregoric" is derived. In a sense these three friends had been a "tonic" to Paul.

Epaphras, mentioned earlier in 1:7 as the founder of the Colossian church and as Paul's representative, is warmly commended in verses 12 and 13. Describing him as *one of you* (v. 12; cf. v. 9) and as *a servant [bondslave] of Christ Jesus* (v. 12), Paul reminds the Colossians that Epaphras continually strives (see 1:29 for the same word) for them in his prayers. The point of his concern is that they may stand firm, mature, fully convinced in reference to the will of God. The allusion is to the danger of wavering under the influence of the heretical teaching being propagated at Colossae.

Verse 13 contains the letter's final reference to Epaphras. In it Paul vouches for Epaphras' anxiety for the Colossians, assuring them that *he hath much labor for you, and for them in Laodicea, and for them in Hierapolis* (ASV).

"Labor," coming from a term which suggests heavy toil, may here denote the emotional distress which Epaphras had experienced in reference to his people at Colossae. The KJV renders it "zeal"; TCNT, "deep interest." "Laodicea" and "Hierapolis" were neighboring cities.

Luke and *Demas* are mentioned next (v. 14). Of the latter no descriptive phrases are used. Of Luke Paul says very little, but interestingly enough, much of what we know about this man is derived from this casual reference to him. It is from this passage, for instance, that we learn that Luke was a physician; and the context suggests that he was a Gentile (cf. v. 11). The adjective "beloved" confirms what is implied in Acts, namely, that Luke was a dear and trusted friend of Paul. Some, pointing to the use of the Greek word for "beloved" in the sense of "only," think the expression "beloved physician" may here mean "my personal physician."

Verse 15 contains greetings for the Christian *brethren* of Laodicea, for *Nymphas* and *the church* meeting *in their house* (ASV). The Greek word for "Nymphas" may be either masculine or feminine, depending on the position of the accent mark. Accordingly, the versions differ. The KJV and ASV, for instance, interpret it to be a man's name. The RSV and NEB have "Nympha," a woman's name. The decision (i.e., whether to construe the name as masculine or as feminine) is made largely on the basis of the pronoun used with "house." At this point, however, the Greek manuscripts exhibit a variety of readings. Instead of "their" house (ASV) some texts have "his" house (cf. KJV); others, "her" house (cf. RSV, NEB). The feminine pronoun perhaps represents the true reading. Numerically the evidence for it is slight, but the overall attestation is very strong. If "their" is accepted as the proper reading, the antecedent must be both "Nymphas" (Nympha) and "the brethren" mentioned earlier in the verse. This makes for a rather awkward construction.

The reference to the church meeting in Nympha's "house" is interesting. There were, of course, no church buildings in apostolic times. In the New Testament "church" always designates an assembly of believers, never the place where they met. In fact, the earliest evidence for "church" in the sense of a building dates from the third century. Similar references to churches meeting in homes are in Romans 16:5; 1 Corinthians 16:9; and Philemon 2.

The location of Nympha's "house-church" is uncertain, though the context implies that it was in the vicinity of Laodicea. Some have suggested that it was in Hierapolis, a city near both Colossae and Laodicea.

3. *Instructions* (vv. 16, 17). The final instructions of the letter concern three matters: (1) the Colossian epistle (v. 16a), (2) the epistle from Laodicea (v. 16b), and (3) counsel for Archippus (v. 17). Brief though the section is, it is of considerable interest for what it tells us about the manner in which Paul's letters were circulated.

The Colossians, after reading this epistle, are to see to it that it is read also in the Laodicean church. Perhaps they would first make a copy of the epistle to keep for themselves and then would send the original to the Laodiceans.

In return, the Colossians were to secure *the epistle from Laodicea* (v. 16b). It has been conjectured that this is the epistle which we know as Ephesians, but that seems highly unlikely. The most obvious conclusion to draw from this reference is that Paul wrote an epistle to the Laodicean church which has not been preserved. A similar reference to a lost letter is in 1 Corinthians 5:9.

Archippus (v. 17), to whom a special message is sent, is mentioned again in Philemon 2, and in a way that suggests he was a member of Philemon's household. Many interpreters think he was Philemon's son. The verse before us implies that he had some ministerial responsibility in the Colossian church, though no definite information is given. Perhaps he was serving as pastor in the absence of Epaphras. At any rate, it was a service *in the Lord* and therefore important.

The church is given the responsibility of exhorting him to *take heed* to his *ministry* ("duty," NEB). Some commentators, assuming that this charge implies a degree of failure on the part of Archippus, interpret it as a rebuke. But it is not sure that censure was intended. This could have been Paul's way of letting the church know that Archippus had his full support.

To *fulfill* a ministry *received in the Lord* is to discharge its obligations to the full. Norlie's paraphrase captures the force of it: "God called you into His service — Oh, do not fail Him!"

4. *Benediction* (v. 18). When a stenographer's services were employed in the writing of a letter (as perhaps was Paul's custom; cf. Rom. 16:22), he was normally left to compose the benediction himself. Paul, however, appears regularly to have written the benediction in his own hand (cf. 2 Thess. 3:17). Accordingly, taking the stylus from the amanuensis, he attaches his signature to this letter: *The salutation of me Paul with mine own hand.*

In doing this the apostle is reminded anew of the chain on his wrist and touchingly adds: *Remember my bonds.*

The letter ends, as it began, with a prayer: *Grace be with you.*

For Further Study

1. Use a concordance to study what the New Testament says about prayer and watchfulness.
2. Study Paul's requests for prayer for himself.
3. Make a list of Paul's commendations of his friends.

PHILEMON

**A STUDY GUIDE
COMMENTARY**

The Epistle to Philemon

Lightfoot describes Philemon as unique among the writings of Paul because it is the only strictly private letter preserved and included in the canon of Holy Scripture (p. 300). The Pastoral Epistles were addressed to individuals but appear to have been intended for public reading. They are concerned with various important matters of church discipline and government. Philemon, however, does not once "touch upon any question of public interest. It is addressed apparently to a layman. It is wholly occupied with an incident of domestic life" (Lightfoot, p. 306). Moreover, it was not written that Paul might exert his apostolic authority over someone but that he might communicate as friend with friend.

The letter to Philemon is closely related to the Colossian letter and to a lesser extent to Ephesians and Philippians. Colossians and Philemon (perhaps also Ephesians and Philippians) were written during the same period of the apostle's life and probably during the same Roman imprisonment (see pages 13 and 14 of this book). Griffith Thomas refers to the suggestion of another that these four letters "give us a great spiritual square: at the top, Colossians—the ideal head, Christ; at the base, Ephesians—the ideal body, the Church; at one side, Philippians—the ideal Christian in relation to the head; and at the other side, Philemon—the ideal Church member in relation to his fellowmembers" (pp. 149-50).

The *occasion* for the letter may be discerned by even a superficial reading of it. A slave named Onesimus had run away from his master, whose name was Philemon. In the providence of God Onesimus made his way to Rome; there, the imprisoned Paul was instrumental in leading Onesimus into a saving knowledge of Christ. In due time the apostle returned Onesimus to his master Philemon with this letter as an appeal to receive Onesimus as a beloved brother. In the letter, Paul even offered to repay any debts that Onesimus might have owed his wronged master.

The *value* of the letter, in spite of its brevity and the absence of doctrinal teaching, is considerable. Its depiction of Christian character, its model of Christian friendship, its portrayal of Christian home life in the first century, and its bearing on the institution of slavery give this epistle a distinctive quality. It has been said that, in a few familiar lines, we have such grace, salt, and trust that this short epistle gleams like a pearl of purity in the rich treasure of the New Testament. It is a pattern of tact, fine feeling, and graciousness that far surpasses all the wisdom of the world. Lightfoot speaks of this short letter as "infinitely precious" (p. 303). "Nowhere," he explains, "is the social influence of the Gospel more strikingly exerted; nowhere does the nobility of the Apostle's character receive a more vivid illustration than in this accidental pleading on behalf of a runaway slave" (p. 306).

The letter may be divided into four parts: salutation (vv. 1-3), thanksgiving and prayer for Philemon (vv. 4-7), the request of Paul on behalf of Onesimus (vv. 8-22), and final greetings (vv. 23-24).

I. SALUTATION (vv. 1-3).

1. *The writer and his associate* (v. 1a). The author of the letter was obviously Paul, though the name of Timothy, his younger companion, is associated with Paul's own name in the opening statement. H. C. G. Moule calls the inclusion of Timothy's name "a touch of delicate courtesy" (*Cambridge Bible*, p. 167). The mention of his name may also reflect that Timothy was known by Philemon and that Timothy had an interest in the case of Onesimus.

Verse 1a. Paul calls himself "a prisoner of Christ Jesus" (ASV). Vincent thinks these words "prepare the way" for Paul's request of Philemon, adding that "the title 'apostle' is laid aside as not befitting a private and friendly letter" (p. 175). But more than that, Paul's designation of himself as a prisoner gives the letter at its outset a tone of remarkable persuasiveness—a *prisoner* pleading the case of a *slave*.

Outwardly and literally Paul was Nero's prisoner; inwardly and spiritually he was a prisoner of Christ (cf. Eph. 3:1; 4:1; 6:20). In thus relating his imprisonment to *Christ Jesus* Paul shuts his eyes to all secondary causes and sees in his captivity the working of an all-wise God. "Christ Himself had riveted his manacles on Paul's wrists; therefore, he bore them as lightly and as proudly as a bride might wear the bracelet that her husband had clasped on her" (Scroggie, p. 12).

Timothy is called "our [lit., the] brother," as elsewhere are Quartus (Rom. 16:23), Sosthenes (1 Cor. 1:1), and Apollos (1 Cor. 16:12). Timothy is never called an apostle. A resident of Lystra (Acts 16:1), he was converted to Christianity under the ministry of Paul on the first visit of the apostle to that city; later, on Paul's second journey, Timothy became a member of the missionary team (Acts 16:3).

2. *The recipients of the letter* (vv. 1b–2). These verses introduce us to three persons, perhaps a family, in the small Phrygian town of Colossae.[1] Although the letter is in the canon and is intended for all believers, it was originally written for these three people.

Verse 1b. Philemon was the principal recipient of the letter; observe the use of the second person singular Greek pronoun throughout the letter (e.g., vv. 2, 4, 5, 6, 7, 8) and the singular "brother" in direct address (vv. 7, 20). He appears to have been a resident of Colossae, since his slave Onesimus is described in the Colossian letter as "one of you" (4:9). This epistle implies that Philemon, like Timothy, was a convert of Paul (v. 19). That he was a prominent member of the Colossian church is indicated by the fact that the congregation met in his house for worship (v. 2b).

Philemon is described as "our [the word apparently includes both Paul and Timothy] beloved friend and fellow-worker" (ASV). "Beloved friend" (*agapētos*) is an adjective used as a substantive. The latter word (*synergos*, fellow worker) appears in the New Testament only in the writings of Paul (e.g., Rom. 16:3, 9, 21; 1 Cor. 3:9; 2 Cor. 1:24; Phil. 2:25; Col. 4:11) and in 3 John 8.

Verse 2a. Apphia may have been the wife of Philemon; this interpretation is supported by the fact that a runaway slave would be a concern to the whole household. The placement of her name immediately after Philemon's rather than after that of Archippus provides additional evidence of her special relation to Philemon. In calling her "our sister" Paul means simply that she was a Christian.

Archippus may have been a son of Philemon and Apphia. The only other New Testament reference to him is in Colossians 4:17, where he is admonished to fulfill the ministry (*diakonia*) that he had received in the Lord (see the commentary on Col. 4:17). It has been inferred from Colossians 4:17 that Archippus held some official position in the Colossian congregation.[2] Onesimus, it is argued, was to be received into the fellowship of the Colossian church, and Archippus would have a significant role to play in this if he were an officer in that church. But it is more probable that Archippus's name is mentioned because he belonged to the household of Philemon and Apphia. However, there may be an element of truth in both of these interpretations.

---

[1]See pp. 9–10 of this volume for a discussion of Colossae.

[2]Lightfoot and others have concluded from the Colossians passage that Archippus was perhaps pastor of the church at Laodicea. The position taken above, however, seems to me to be correct.

Archippus is designated as the "fellow soldier" of Paul and Timothy. The term is used only here and in Philippians 2:25; it is a reminder of the fact that the Christian life involves spiritual warfare (cf. Eph. 6:10ff.). The NEB renders it here "our comrade-in-arms." Vincent comments that in using the word of Archippus, Paul recognized his younger friend "as a fellow-campaigner in the gospel warfare" (p. 176), and adds that the imagery "may have been suggested by Paul's military associations in Rome" (p. 177).

Verse 2b. The letter was intended not only for the three persons named above but also for "the church" that met at the house of Philemon (lit. "the according-to-your-house church"). There were no church buildings in New Testament times, and large cities might have had several "house" churches (congregations).[3] It is probable that a small town such as Colossae would have only one such congregation. For other references to "house" churches, see Romans 16:5; 1 Corinthians 16:19; and Colossians 4:15.

That the whole church should be included in the address of this otherwise private letter is indicative of the importance of the subject matter and of the fact that the handling of Onesimus's situation affected the entire church, not just the household of Philemon.

3. *The greeting* (v. 3). The greeting, which is essentially a prayer, is identical to the greetings in Romans, 1 and 2 Corinthians, Galatians, and Ephesians. Similar greetings are given in Colossians and 1 and 2 Thessalonians.

The two elements in this greeting are grace and peace. Scroggie defines the former as "a disposition in the Divine nature" and says it "stands for the whole sum of the unmerited blessings which come to men through Jesus Christ" (p. 20). Vincent describes it as "the free, spontaneous, absolute lovingkindness of God towards men" (p. 4). Peace, the second element, has a deeper meaning than mere tranquillity. At its root is the idea of reconciliation but added to this is the notion of general well-being.

II. THANKSGIVING AND PRAYER FOR PHILEMON (vv. 4-7).

The greetings in Paul's epistles are regularly followed by thanksgiving or doxology; the most notable exception is Galatians. The to-

---

[3]The earliest references to church buildings date from the beginning of the third century, in the writings of Clement of Alexandria and Hippolytus. See the special note in Vincent, pp. 193-194. Lightfoot, in a note on Colossians 4:15, writes: "There is no clear example of a separate building set apart for Christian worship within the limits of the Roman empire before the third century, though apartments in private houses might be specially devoted to this purpose" (p. 243).

pics of discussion in these verses are not really difficult to isolate, but some of the details "are dislocated and inverted in the struggle of the several ideas for immediate utterance" (Lightfoot, p. 334). The following paraphrase by Lightfoot provides insight into the meaning of the whole:

> I never cease to give thanks to my God for thy well-doing, and thou art ever mentioned in my prayers. For they tell me of thy love and faith—thy faith which thou hast in the Lord Jesus, and thy love which thou showest towards all the saints; and it is my prayer that this active sympathy and charity, thus springing from thy faith, may abound more and more, as thou attainest to the perfect knowledge of every good thing bestowed upon us by God, looking unto and striving after Christ. For indeed it gave me great joy and comfort to hear of thy loving-kindness, and to learn how the hearts of God's people had been cheered and refreshed by thy help, my dear brother.

This paraphrase shows that verses 4-7 contain three movements: thanksgiving (vv. 4-5), petition (v. 6), and affirmation (v. 7). It is not easy to distinguish the three elements. Scroggie remarks that "the Apostle's heart is so full that his words have not time to form logical sequence" (p. 27).

Verse 4. Paul's gratitude and intercessory prayer for Philemon is probably best rendered, "I always thank my God when I make mention of you in [at the time of] my prayers." The pronoun "you," a singular form in Greek, is a reference to Philemon. That the very mention (or remembrance) of his name elicits an expression of gratitude to God is a commentary both on the noble character of Philemon and on Paul's profound appreciation for him. The use of the word "mention" in this context suggests intercession, which is developed in verse 6. "Prayer" (*proseuchē*) includes any type of worshipful approach to God.

Verse 5. The reason for Paul's thanksgiving is expressed in this way: "Because I continue [present tense] to hear [probably through Epaphras, Col. 1:7-8; 4:12, and possibly from Onesimus] of the love and faith that you have toward [*pros*] the Lord Jesus and to [*eis*] all the saints." This is an apparently simple verse, but a question arises when it is carefully analyzed: Are both the love and the faith directed toward both the Lord Jesus *and* His people "the saints"? The position of the Greek pronoun for "your" may suggest an affirmative answer. The NEB accordingly reads, "your love and faith towards the Lord Jesus and towards all God's people" (cf. the similar translation of the NASB). But what does "faith" (*pistis*) mean? Presumably in this interpretation it must mean fidelity or reliability of character rather than saving faith. Moffatt translates it "loyalty."

Lightfoot, perhaps representing the majority of interpreters, opts for the view that faith is directed toward the Lord Jesus and love is directed toward His people (cf. his paraphrase quoted above). The NIV reflects this interpretation: "your faith in the Lord Jesus and your love for all the saints." The use of two different prepositions in Greek (*pros* before "the Lord Jesus" and *eis* before "all the saints") lends support to this interpretation.

C. F. D. Moule, who argues for this interpretation, points out that the passage is "chiastic" in structure (i.e., *chi*-shaped, as in x-y-y-x [x] love [y] faith [y] Lord [x] saints). Scroggie, taking the same view, calls it an "inverted parallelism." "Thus we have, as it were, faith towards the Lord Jesus imbedded in the center of the verse, while 'thy love . . . toward all the saints,' which flows from it, wraps it round" (p. 29).

Verse 6. This verse, the most obscure in the letter, seems to state the substance[4] of Paul's prayers for Philemon: that his love and faith (just mentioned), which give such aid and comfort to God's people generally, may be extended to the special case of Onesimus. In Lumby's words: "that Philemon might add to the other tokens of his true faith, this further one, to receive Onesimus" (p. 623).

The critical words are "communication" (*koinōnia;* ASV, fellowship), "effectual" (*energēs*), "knowledge" (KJV, "by the acknowledging"; *en epignōsei.,* lit., "in knowledge"), and "in Christ" (*eis Christon,* lit., "unto [or, in reference to] Christ"). There is considerable difference of opinion as to the meanings of these terms and how they are related within the sentence. The word the KJV renders "communication" (*koinōnia*) basically denotes having things in common and is usually translated "participation" or "fellowship" (cf. ASV).[5] "The fellowship of thy faith" (ASV) could mean Philemon's fellowship with Christ by faith (faith as the bond of fellowship), the fellowship in faith that he shares with other Christians or with Paul (faith as the sphere of fellowship), or the communication/sharing of his faith to/with others (faith as the thing shared; cf. NIV).

---

[4]Vincent thinks the verse gives not the substance but the purpose of Paul's prayers for Philemon. In the final analysis the two ideas overlap in a context such as this, and it is difficult to insist on a rigid distinction. Lightfoot, in fact, combines both ideas, explaining that the verse gives "the aim and purport of St. Paul's prayer" (p. 335).

[5]The word is used by Paul to speak of the Christian's sharing with Christ (1 Cor. 1:9; 10:16; Phil. 3:10), with the Holy Spirit (2 Cor. 13:13; Phil. 2:1), with fellow Christians (Rom. 15:27), and in various Christian works (Phil. 1:5; 4:14). Sometimes it is used of a contribution of money or goods (Rom. 12:13; 15:26, 27; 2 Cor. 8:4, 9:13, etc.).

Fellowship or sharing may also mean almsgiving or performing deeds of kindness that arise from faith. In this interpretation faith is viewed as motivating the sharing of material things with those in need. All these interpretations are grammatically possible.

The RSV interprets "effectual" (*energēs*, active, effective, operative, powerful) in the sense of "promoting": "I pray that the sharing of your faith may promote the knowledge of all the good that is ours in Christ." The NIV interprets the same word as "active": "I pray that you may be active in sharing your faith, so that you will have a full understanding of every good thing we have in Christ." Vincent understands the word to mean "prove," "show to be effectual." The NASB uses "effective": ". . . that the fellowship of your faith may become effective through the knowledge of every good thing," etc.

The word for "knowledge" denotes full or mature knowledge and is characteristic of the Prison Epistles. The NIV renders it "full understanding." The NASB translation (see above) takes knowledge to be the means by which the fellowship of Philemon's faith would become effective. Vincent sees it here as the sphere or element in which the fellowship of Philemon's faith "will develop to the greatest advantage of others, including Onesimus. The larger his knowledge of [every good thing], the more will he be moved to deal kindly and Christianly. He will recognize through this knowledge the rightness of Paul's request" (p. 180).

The last phrase ("unto Christ") may mean "unto Christ's glory—the advancement of his cause" (Vincent, p. 181). Or the phrase may be taken with the words "every good thing that is in us." In this interpretation the Greek should be understood as equivalent to "in Christ" (ordinarily expressed in Paul by *en Christō*). This meaning is given by RSV, NIV, and others. It is implied by NEB: "All the blessings that our *union with Christ* brings us" (italics mine). The NASB translates the phrase to mean "for Christ's sake," but the precise relation of these words to the rest of the sentence is unclear.

To sum up, there appear to be two ideas in this verse: On the one hand there is Paul's desire that the fellowship of Philemon's faith may become active and effective, abounding more and more; on the other hand there is the good that will result from this, namely, a fuller understanding of the benefits that belong to us in Christ.

Verse 7. This verse, which affirms the noble and generous character of Philemon, gives the reason for the thanksgiving mentioned in verses 4 and 5; namely, the joy and consolation (encouragement) that the apostle had received from the news of Philemon's loving ministry among the Colossian Christians.

The "bowels" (lit. viscera or entrails; cf. Acts 1:18) of the saints or the people of God refers figuratively to the seat of the emotions; the NIV has "hearts" (see also vv. 12, 20). "Are refreshed" (*anapauō*, cause to rest, refresh) may mean relief from pain and sorrow. Vincent says the dominant idea is "refreshment in contrast with weariness from toil" (p. 181). This word was used by Christ when He promised that those who were weary and overburdened would, in coming to Him, be given "rest" (Matt. 11:28-29).

It probably never occurred to Philemon that his loving deeds that refreshed the hearts of the Colossian Christians would bring joy and encouragement to his friend Paul, imprisoned in faraway Rome. But as a pebble that has been cast into a lake sends out widening circles, so "the smallest deeds and words, good or bad, have an expanding influence. What is done or said here may be carried by the winds like seeds to the ends of the earth, to make or mar, to gladden or sadden other souls" (Scroggie, p. 34).

III. THE REQUEST OF PAUL IN BEHALF OF ONESIMUS (vv. 8-22).

These verses contain the heart of the letter. In them one should note the tactful way Paul appealed to his friend Philemon, the subtle hint of the authority to which Paul was entitled although he was unwilling to use it, and the gentle reminder that Philemon had a great moral obligation to his friend Paul. The whole tone of the appeal suggests that Paul did not expect to be refused. The passage expresses the basis of Paul's request (vv. 8-9), the statement of his request (vv. 10-11), and an expansion of his request (vv. 12-22).

1. *The basis of Paul's request* (vv. 8-9).
Verses 8-9. The thought of these verses is, "I do not appeal to you in my capacity as an apostle nor on the basis of authority but simply as a Christian brother who has a genuine concern for all the persons involved." Upon examining the details, we detect that Paul based his appeal on two considerations. The primary basis was love (vv. 8-9a); the other had to do with the adverse conditions under which Paul was living at the time (v. 9b).

Two expressions bring out the idea of love as a compelling reason for granting Paul's request. The first is the "wherefore" (v. 8), which points back to the preceding paragraph and Philemon's love. In effect the word says, "I know of your love and I now appeal to it." The "wherefore" perhaps also alludes to Paul's prayer for Philemon (expressed in the preceding verses) and affirms Paul's confidence that that prayer will be answered. The apostle is sure that God will remind Philemon of his Christian responsibility in the matter at hand and will direct him to perform it with characteristic generosity and kindness. For this reason Paul does not command but entreats, although his apostolic office and Philemon's debt to him for his conversion (v. 19) would warrant a command for cooperation.

That love is the primary ground of Paul's appeal is expressly stated in the words "for love's sake." This love could be the love of Paul for Philemon and Onesimus or Philemon's love for Paul, but perhaps the term should be interpreted *absolutely*. It is, in Lightfoot's words, "love regarded as a principle of action" (p. 337).

A secondary basis of Paul's appeal is found in the description of himself as "Paul the aged" (or, "Paul, an old man")[6] and "a prisoner of Christ Jesus." The language is very touching, and would surely have elicited tender feelings from his friend. Perhaps Paul felt that if the simple, unadorned appeal to love should fail, these references to his advanced age and forced confinement would add another powerful dimension to his appeal.

2. *The statement of Paul's request* (vv. 10-11).

Verse 10. Verses 8 and 9 were prefatory; next comes the request. Paul speaks in behalf of his spiritual "child,"[7] Onesimus,[8] who is mentioned by name here for the first time in the letter. We are not told how Paul met the delinquent slave but simply that he had "be-

---

[6]The RSV renders a Greek text which uses the word *presbeutēs*, meaning "ambassador," and in a footnote explains that the word used in the best Greek manuscripts *(presbutēs)* generally means "old man." The word for ambassador *(presbeutēs)* differs from it by the addition of a single letter. Lightfoot thinks "ambassador" is the correct word, contending that the two words *(presbutēs* and *presbeutēs)* simply represent variant spellings and that both could mean either "old," or "ambassador." If this should be the proper rendering, it would be "a quiet reminder, in the act of entreaty, that the suppliant was no ordinary one; he was the Lord's envoy, dignified by suffering for the Lord" (H. C. G. Moule, *Cambridge Bible*, p. 172).

There is no way of knowing Paul's exact age at the time of this writing. He was a young man at the time of Stephen's martyrdom (Acts 7:58), and is generally thought to have been about sixty when this epistle was written. Vincent suggests that Paul may have aged prematurely under the rigors of his missionary endeavors. H. C. G. Moule appropriately remarks that "at all periods men have called themselves old when they felt so" (*Cambridge Bible*, p. 172).

[7]One should not fail to catch the significance of this designation. Paul might have referred to Onesimus as the "slave" of Philemon; he chose rather to call him his own "child." It is an indication of Paul's earnest and deep love.

[8]A common slave name meaning "profitable." The Greek could be translated, "whom I have begotten . . . *as Onesimus,*" suggesting that it was Paul who gave the runaway slave a new name to symbolize his new character.

gotten" him in the Lord while in bondage. The time reference is to the first Roman imprisonment (A.D. 60-63).

Verse 11. This verse, which is almost parenthetical, involves a play on the meaning of the slave's name (see note at v. 10). The word "unprofitable" may imply that in running away Onesimus had stolen from his master. All that is past now; God's grace has made Onesimus true to his name, so that he is "useful" both to Philemon and to Paul.

Having stated his appeal for Onesimus (vv. 10-11), Paul will now add greater detail (vv. 12-22).

3. *An expansion of Paul's request* (vv. 12-22).

Verses 12-13. Paul emphasizes three things: (1) the decision to send Onesimus back to Philemon, (2) the affection that the apostle had for the runaway slave,[9] and (3) his desire to keep Onesimus at his side as a fellow servant.

The words "that in thy stead he might have ministered unto me" (v. 13) make it seem "almost as though Philemon had *sent* Onesimus to serve Paul, instead of having lost him as a runaway" (H. K. Moulton, p. 74).

Verse 14. Paul, in spite of his inclination to keep Onesimus with him, was unwilling to act without the consent of Philemon in the matter. Whatever was done, the apostle wanted it to be according to the will of his friend. Lightfoot, drawing upon the significance of the particle "as," thinks the latter part of the verse shows that Paul did not want Philemon's action to have even the *appearance* of constraint. Whatever favor he did for Onesimus was to be entirely spontaneous, not forced.

Verse 15. The statement of this verse, suggesting that Onesimus's departure from his master may have been within the larger will of God, is reminiscent of the words of Joseph in Genesis 45:5-8. Paul does not assert this dogmatically but represents it simply as a possibility. Vincent paraphrases it thus: "It might be that God allowed the slave to leave you in order that he might become a Christian disciple; and if I should retain him, you would not have him back in your household as a Christian brother." The same author then explains: "Philemon's attention is thus turned from his [Onesimus's] wrongs to the providential economy which has made these wrongs work for good" (p. 188).

Verse 16. Paul does not say that Onesimus would no longer *be* a

---

[9]"Mine own bowels" means, in today's language, "my very heart" (see discussion of verse 7). The NEB interprets Paul's words to mean, "I am sending a part of myself."

slave, but that Philemon was no longer to *regard* him as a slave. "Beloved brother" means fellow Christian, dearly loved.

Verse 17 expresses the main point of the letter—namely, that Philemon will give to Onesimus a kindly reception (a thought foreshadowed in vv. 10-11). Paul has prepared the way for this request by various considerations: (1) his close relationship with Philemon, (2) his explanation of what God had done for Onesimus, and (3) the new value of Onesimus both to the apostle and to Philemon. All of this is alluded to in the "therefore" of this verse.

Verse 18 needs little explanation. Paul simply offers to make restitution for any debts Onesimus may have incurred. It is not clear whether the runaway had actually robbed his master, but such may be implied. If theft is not suggested, the statement may allude to the loss suffered by Philemon when deprived of the service of his slave.

Verse 19. "I Paul write [an epistolary aorist in Greek] it with mine own hand" leads some interpreters to conclude that this entire letter was written by Paul without the aid of an amanuensis. Others think the apostle is asserting only that he wrote the first half of verse 19 with his own hand. The latter interpretation is perhaps to be preferred.

What is written here is tantamount to Paul's promissory note, which the Greeks called a *cheirographon* (lit., a handwriting; cf. Col. 4:18), meaning an autographed "IOU" (cf. C. F. D. Moule, p. 148).

The words "thou owest unto me even thine own self besides" are a reminder to Philemon that humanly speaking his conversion came about through the ministry of Paul.[10] The idea is: "Even if you remit the debt as I am requesting, you will still owe me yourself."

Verse 20. Lightfoot sees a note of pathos in the use of "brother" in the entreaty of this verse. It shows, he says, that the verse is an affectionate appeal "of a brother to a brother on behalf of a brother" (p. 344). In the Greek behind the words "I do wish . . . that I may have some benefit" (NIV; ASV, "let me have joy") the personal pronoun is emphatic; Paul identifies the interests of Onesimus with his own. Lightfoot's paraphrase expresses it well: "I seem to be entreating for Onesimus; but I am pleading for *myself:* the favour will be done to me" (p. 344). The Greek verb (*oninēmi*) is an aorist optative form used only here in the New Testament, and means "to benefit, to profit, to have joy" (cf. NIV and ASV renderings given

[10]If Philemon was converted through Paul's ministry—and this text seems to imply that he was—his conversion occurred somewhere other than at Colossae, for Paul had not visited Colossae.

above). Its use in extrabiblical writings may lend support to the view that it here has a connotation of filial responsibility. Lightfoot, who suggests this, paraphrases it: "May I receive such a return from thee, as a father has a right to expect from his child" (p. 344). For "refresh my heart in Christ" (NIV) see the discussion of verse 7, where Paul affirms that Philemon had refreshed the hearts of the saints. The appeal in the present verse is for relief from anxiety.

Verses 21-22. The central part of the epistle closes with (1) a restatement of Paul's confidence in Philemon, (2) a request that his Colossian friend provide a lodging place (*xenia,* "guest room"; or more frequently, "hospitality" or "entertainment") for him for a projected visit to Colossae, and (3) an expression of the apostle's expectation of a release from prison that will permit him to visit Philemon (cf. Phil. 2:24). Lightfoot sees in this mention of a personal visit to Colossae "a gentle compulsion." "The Apostle would thus be able to see for himself that Philemon had not disappointed his expectations" (p. 345).

Looking back over the section that began at verse 8, Harold K. Moulton writes that "one could hardly find an appeal based on more varied . . . grounds" (p. 75). These include love (vv. 8–9), divine overruling (vv. 15–16), the sense of partnership between Paul and Philemon (v. 17), an offer to make up financial loss (vv. 18–19a), a reminder of Philemon's indebtedness to the apostle (v. 19b), the desire for a friend's help in relieving anxiety (v. 20), and an expression of confidence in Philemon's obedience (v. 21).

IV. FINAL GREETINGS (VV. 23–25).

The names mentioned here all appear in the Colossian letter, and thus constitute evidence of the close relationship of that letter to this one.

Verses 23-24. For Epaphras, see the discussion of Colossians 1:7–8; 4:12. For Mark, Aristarchus, Demas, and Luke, see the discussion of Colossians 4:10, 14.

Verse 25. The benediction reverts to the plural pronoun to include Apphia, Archippus, and the whole church that met at Philemon's house (cf. v. 2). It is a prayer for grace, with all the fullness of blessing that it brings, to be with the spirit of all of these Christian friends (cf. Gal. 6:18).

Luther's appraisal of the letter to Philemon may serve as an appropriate conclusion to our study:

> This epistle showeth a right noble lovely example of Christian love. Here we see how St Paul layeth himself out for poor Onesimus, and with all his means pleadeth his cause with his master: and so setteth

himself as if he were Onesimus, and had himself done wrong to Philemon. Even as Christ did for us with God the Father, thus also doth St Paul for Onesimus with Philemon. . . . We are all his Onesimi, to my thinking. (Quoted by Lightfoot, pp. 317-318).

Bibliography

Abbott, T. K., "The Epistles to the Ephesians and to the Colossians" in *The International Critical Commentary* (Edinburgh: T. & T. Clark, n.d.).

Barclay, William, "The Letters to the Philippians, Colossians, and Thessalonians" in the *Daily Study Bible* (Philadelphia: Westminster Press, 1959).

Beare, F. W., "The Epistle to the Colossians" in *The Interpreter's Bible* (New York: Abingdon Press, 1955).

Bruce, F. F., "Commentary on the Epistles to the Ephesians and the Colossians" in *The New International Commentary on the New Testament* (Grand Rapids: Wm. B. Eerdmans Publishing Co., 1957).

Calvin, John, *Commentaries on the Epistles to the Philippians, Colossians and Thessalonians*. Translated and edited by John Pringle. Reprint Edition (Grand Rapids: Wm. B. Eerdmans Publishing Co., 1948).

Daille, John, *An Exposition of the Epistle to the Colossians*. Reprint Edition (Marshallton, Delaware: The National Foundation for Christian Education, n.d.).

Dargan, E. C. "The Epistle to the Colossians" in *An American Commentary* (Philadelphia: The American Baptist Publication Society, n.d.).

Eadie, John, *Commentary on the Epistle of Paul to the Colossians*. Reprint Edition (Grand Rapids: Zondervan Publishing House, n.d.).

Ellicott, C. J., *A Critical and Grammatical Commentary on St. Paul's Epistles to the Philippians, Colossians, and to Philemon* (London: John W. Parker and Son, 1857).

Findlay, George G., "Colossians" in *The Pulpit Bible* (New York: Funk and Wagnalls, n.d.).

Gross, Alexander, "The Epistles to the Colossians and the Ephesians" in the *Bible for Home and School* (New York: The Macmillan Co., 1910).

Lightfoot, J. B., *St. Paul's Epistles to the Colossians and to Phile-*

mon. Reprint Edition (Grand Rapids: Zondervan Publishing House, 1959).

Lumby, Rawson, "Philemon" in *A Popular Introduction to the New Testament*. Vol. 3. Edited by Philip Schaff (New York: Scribner, 1882).

Maclaren, Alexander, "The Epistles of St. Paul to the Colossians and Philemon" in *The Expositor's Bible* (New York: Hodder and Stoughton, n.d.).

Macphail, S. R., "The Epistle to the Colossians" in *Handbook for Bible Classes and Private Students* (Edinburgh: T. & T. Clark, 1911).

Moffatt, James, "The Epistles of Paul to the Colossians, to Philemon and to the Ephesians" in *The Moffatt New Testament Commentary* (London: Hodder and Stoughton, 1946).

Moule, C. F. D., "The Epistles of Paul the Apostle to the Colossians and to Philemon" in *Cambridge Greek Testament Commentary* (Cambridge: University Press, 1957).

Moule, H. C. G., *Colossian Studies* (New York: Hodder and Stoughton, n.d.).

Moule, H. C. G., "The Epistles of Paul to the Colossians and to Philemon" in *The Cambridge Bible for Schools and Colleges* (Cambridge: University Press, 1932).

Moulton, Harold K., "Colossians, Philemon, and Ephesians" in *Epworth Preacher's Commentaries* (London: Epworth Press, n.d.).

Nicholson, W. R., *Oneness With Christ: Popular Studies in the Epistle to the Colossians*. Reprint edition. (Grand Rapids: Kregel Publications, 1951).

Peake, A. S., "The Epistle to the Colossians" in *The Expositor's Greek Testament*. Reprint Edition (Grand Rapids: Wm. B. Eerdmans Publishing Co., n.d.).

Radford, Lewis B., "The Epistle to the Colossians" in *Westminster Commentaries* (London: Methuen and Co., Ltd., 1931).

Robertson, A. T., *Paul and the Intellectuals*. Revised and edited by W. C. Strickland (Nashville: Broadman Press, 1959).

Scroggie, W. Graham, *Studies in Philemon*. Reprint Edition (Grand Rapids: Kregel Publications, 1977).

Thomas, W. H. Griffith, *Studies in Colossians and Philemon* (Grand Rapids: Baker Book House, 1973).

Vincent, Marvin R., *The Epistles to the Philippians and to Philemon* in "The International Critical Commentary" (Edinburgh: T. & T. Clark, 1897).

All Scriptures, unless otherwise identified, are quoted from the King James Version. Other translations referred to are as follows:

Goodspeed, Edgar J., *The New Testament: An American Translation* (Chicago: The University of Chicago Press, 1951).

Good News for Modern Man: The New Testament in Today's English Version (New York: American Bible Society, n.d.). Referred to in the Study Guide as TEV.

The Holy Bible: American Standard Edition (New York: Thomas Nelson and Sons, 1929). Referred to in the Study Guide as ASV.

The Holy Bible: The Berkeley Version in Modern English (Grand Rapids: Zondervan Publishing House, 1959).

The Holy Bible: The New International Version (Grand Rapids: Zondervan Publishing House, 1978) Referred to in the Study Guide as NIV.

The Holy Bible: Revised Standard Version (New York: National Council of Churches in Christ, 1952). Referred to in the Study Guide as RSV.

Moffatt, James, *The New Testament: A New Translation* (New York: Harper and Brothers, 1950).

The New English Bible (Oxford and Cambridge: University Press, 1964). Referred to in the Study Guide as NEB.

Norlie, Olaf M., *The New Testament: A New Translation* (Grand Rapids: Zondervan Publishing House, 1961).

Phillips, J. B., *The New Testament in Modern English* (New York: The Macmillan Company, 1962).

The Twentieth Century New Testament: A Translation into Modern English (Chicago: Moody Press, n.d.). Referred to in the Study Guide as TCNT.

Weymouth, Richard Francis, *The New Testament in Modern Speech*. Newly revised by James Alexander Robertson (New York: Harper and Brothers, n.d.).

Williams, Charles B., *The New Testament: A Private Translation in the Language of the People* (Chicago: Moody Press, 1949).

ORDER
STUDY GUIDE COMMENTARIES

The Ideal Bible Teacher's Commentary Series

Old Testament

- ☐ Genesis (Wood) — 34743-2 $3.50
- ☐ Exodus (Huey) — 36053-6 $3.50
- ☐ Leviticus (Goldberg) — 41813-5 $3.50
- ☐ Job (Garland) — 24863-9 $2.95
- ☐ Isaiah (Garland) — 24853-1 $3.50
- ☐ Daniel (Wood) — 34723-8 $3.50
- ☐ Amos (Garland) — 24833-7 $2.95
- ☐ Hosea (Garland) — 24843-4 $3.50
- ☐ Malachi (Isbell) — 41673-6 $3.50

New Testament

- ☐ Matthew (Vos) — 33883-2 $2.95
- ☐ Mark (Vos) — 33873-5 $2.95
- ☐ Luke (Gideon) — 24973-2 $3.50
- ☐ John (Hobbs) — 26113-9 $2.95
- ☐ Acts (Vaughan) — 33513-2 $2.95
- ☐ Romans (Vaughan/Corley) — 33573-6 $3.50
- ☐ Galatians (Vaughan) — 33543-4 $2.95
- ☐ Ephesians (Vaughan) — 33533-7 $3.50
- ☐ Philippians (Vos) — 33863-8 $2.95
- ☐ Colossians and Philemon (Vaughan) — 33523-X $3.50
- ☐ Thessalonians (Walvoord) — 34071-3 $2.95
- ☐ Pastoral Epistles, The (Blaiklock) — 21233-2 $3.50
- ☐ James (Vaughan) — 33553-1 $3.50
- ☐ I, II, III John (Vaughan) — 33563-9 $3.50

Prices subject to change without notice

Purchase them at your local bookstore or use this handy coupon for ordering:

Please send me the books I have checked above. I am enclosing $_____
(please add $1.00 to cover postage and handling). Send check or money
order—no cash or C.O.D's please.

Mr./Mrs./Miss _____

Address _____

City _____ State _____ Zip _____

Please allow 3 weeks for delivery.

Zondervan Retail Marketing Services
1420 Robinson Rd., S.E.
Grand Rapids, MI 49506

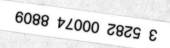